MOM and DAD,
We Need to Talk

MOM and DAD, We Need to Talk

HOW TO HAVE ESSENTIAL CONVERSATIONS WITH YOUR PARENTS ABOUT THEIR FINANCES

Cameron Huddleston

WILEY

Published by John Wiley & Sons, Inc., Hoboken, New Jersey.

Published simultaneously in Canada.

For general information on our other products and services or for technical support, please contact our Customer Care Department within the United States at (800) 762–2974, outside the United States at (317) 572–3993, or fax (317) 572–4002.

Wiley publishes in a variety of print and electronic formats and by print-on-demand. Some material included with standard print versions of this book may not be included in e-books or in print-on-demand. If this book refers to media such as a CD or DVD that is not included in the version you purchased, you may download this material at http://booksupport.wiley .com. For more information about Wiley products, visit www.wiley.com.

Library of Congress Cataloging-in-Publication Data is Available:

ISBN 978-1-119-53836-3 (Hardcover)
ISBN 978-1-119-53843-1 (ePDF)
ISBN 978-1-119-53841-7 (ePub)

COVER DESIGN & ILLUSTRATION: PAUL MCCARTHY

Printed in the United States of America

V10010089_052019

For my mom

Contents

INTRODUCTION

Why the Money Talk Is Essential

There's a good chance you recognize the importance of talking to your parents about their finances if you bought this book – or are thinking about it. But if you're not entirely convinced that you should discuss how they plan to support themselves in retirement, whether they'll be able to afford long-term care if they need it, or if they have a will, let me share a story that might persuade you.

Once upon a time, I didn't realize how essential it was to have detailed conversations with my mom about her finances. It wasn't that I was afraid to bring up money issues with her. After all, I'm comfortable with the topic because I've been a personal finance journalist for more than 15 years. And my mom didn't treat money as a taboo topic, even though plenty of other people in her generation (including my dad) did.

But as she was approaching retirement, I was busy working, having kids, and getting my own financial house in order. I knew that my mom, for the most part, was on top of her finances. She wasn't a big spender. She owned her house outright and lived comfortably. So I didn't foresee her having any financial woes once she retired or as she aged. That doesn't mean, though, I shouldn't have taken the time out of my busy schedule to chat with her about her plans for her future and what she had in place to ensure a comfortable retirement.

To my credit, I did suggest that my mom look into long-term care insurance right around the time my husband and I moved from Washington, D.C., to my hometown in 2003. She and my father had divorced several years before then, so she didn't have the benefit of a spouse to help care for her if dementia or another condition left her unable to care for herself later in life. A long-term care policy would help ensure that her care would be paid for if she needed it.

So she took my advice and talked to an insurance agent. But no long-term care insurance provider was willing to give her a policy because she was considered too high risk. She had an acoustic neuroma – a noncancerous tumor that developed on the nerve from her inner ear to her brain – which she had opted to have treated with radiation rather than surgically removed.

When she told me she couldn't get long-term care coverage, I should have used that opportunity to sit down with her and review all of her sources of income to figure out whether she could pay for care on her own if she ever needed it. But I dropped the ball.

As fate would have it, my mom started showing signs that she was having trouble remembering things. Of course, not wanting to think the worst, I initially assumed that she was asking the same questions more than once and repeating things because she had lost her hearing in her left ear as a result of the acoustic neuroma. But one night while I was at her house, it became painfully obvious that her hearing loss wasn't the problem.

She asked me if I wanted to see a new bench she had bought for her patio. We went outside, looked at the bench, then went back in and started talking. Within a few minutes, she asked, "Do you want to see the new bench I got for my patio?" My heart sank.

At that point, there was no denying that my mom's short-term memory was fading. I should've acted quickly to ask her to make a list of all of her financial accounts, to make sure her legal documents such as her will were updated, and to discuss how to pay for long-term care because it was no longer a question of *if* she would need it but *when*.

I should have, but I didn't.

I recognized the need for having a conversation then. But I was afraid – not of talking to my mom about her finances but of saying that we needed to have a conversation because she was starting to forget things. I didn't want to be the one to tell her that she was losing her memory.

I ended up calling her primary-care doctor, whom I knew, and asked if he'd be willing to suggest at her next appointment that she be tested for dementia. To my great relief, he did. My mom then met with a neurologist and took a test. But she told me that the neurologist said the results of the test didn't show that she had dementia.

I wasn't convinced. I also knew I couldn't wait any longer to start getting involved in my mom's finances. The first step was getting her to set up an appointment with an attorney to update her legal documents – her will, living will, and power of attorney. It was especially important to get those latter two documents drafted. Her living will named my sister and me as her health care surrogates and gave us authority to make health care decisions for her. And we both were named her power of attorney, which gave us the right to make financial decisions for her.

You're probably thinking, "This story's not so bad. It all eventually worked out."

It almost didn't.

For estate planning documents to be valid, you have to be mentally competent when you sign them. Around the time my mom signed hers, she had visited another neurologist, taken more tests and was diagnosed with Alzheimer's disease. Fortunately, she was still aware enough of what was going on that the attorney found her competent to sign her will, living will, and power of attorney documents.

If I had waited any longer to encourage my mom to meet with an attorney, she might not have been able to sign those documents. Then I would've spent a lot of time and money in the court system getting conservatorship – the legal right to access her accounts and manage her finances for her.

This happened to someone I know. Doug didn't have power of attorney for his father and couldn't get it when he needed it because his dad's dementia had progressed too far. While his father was in the hospital recovering from surgery to repair a bleeding ulcer, Doug couldn't pay his dad's bills because the bank wouldn't give him access to his account without power of attorney. So Doug spent nine months and $10,000 to become conservator for his dad. He had to hire a lawyer and have his dad evaluated by a neuropsychiatrist to prove in court that his dad was incompetent. To become conservator, Doug also had to pass credit and background checks and be interviewed by a court-appointed investigator (a process I explain in detail in Chapter 4).

"The irony is you spend all those thousands of dollars, and it's only good for a year," Doug said. Every year, he had to check in with the court, produce a net-worth statement for his dad, and file a report showing all of his expenses and how he spent his dad's money.

I certainly dodged a bullet there. But because I had waited to get details about my mom's finances until she really needed help, I had a bigger problem. I had to gather information from someone who was having trouble remembering things. It was like trying to put together a puzzle without knowing what the final picture was supposed to be.

Going through her files, I could see my mom's mental decline. Her receipts and documents for her tax returns were no longer neatly organized as they had been in years past. Mail was piling up on the dining room table, and I wasn't sure bills were getting paid. And there were letters – so many letters – requesting donations from groups I knew she had no ties to but clearly she had given money to because they were thanking her and asking her for more.

Because she no longer had a firm grasp of where all of her money was, one of her accounts slipped under my radar. I didn't find out she had $50,000 worth of investments until a notice arrived that her account was about to be turned over to the state treasury department. That was only a couple of years ago, and my mom already was in an assisted living facility. Fortunately, I was able to get the money (because I have power of attorney) and use it to pay for almost a year's worth of care.

Even more stressful than sorting out my mom's finances was making the decision to move her to an assisted-living facility. I discussed it with her at the time, but those conversations were forgotten shortly after they happened. If I had talked to her about what sort of care she wanted and whether she was okay with the idea of living someplace where she could get round-the-clock care from professionals *before* she started losing her memory, I would have felt less stress and guilt when I made the decision for her.

I shared some of this story while being interviewed for a podcast with the credit reporting agency Experian. I wasn't brought on the show specifically to talk about my situation with my mom, but the conversation quickly turned to the topic and remained there for the rest of the interview. Both of the hosts – one man who was slightly older than I am and one man who was younger – wanted to know how they could start having conversations with their parents about their finances. After the interview ended, the two other people in the room at the time stopped me to say that they, too, were going to need to start talking to their parents and wanted to know how.

That's when I realized I needed to help others do what I should've done a lot sooner with my mom: have essential money conversations with their parents. I wish there had been somebody to give me the kick in the pants I needed to start talking to my mom about her finances well before she started losing her memory. I was only 35 when she was diagnosed with Alzheimer's; my mom was 65. I didn't have any friends my age whose parents already were having memory issues or needing help with their finances. So I navigated the difficult process of talking to my mom about money issues on my own and eventually took over management of her finances.

Now, many of my friends are facing the same situation I was in 10 years ago. They're seeing signs that their parents or in-laws need help and are asking me what to do. I'm happy to report that those who have taken my advice and have had conversations with their parents have had success. Their parents have listened and taken action by giving their children details about their finances or contacting attorneys to draft or update estate planning documents.

I can't promise that talking to your parents about all of the financial issues they'll face as they age will be easy. But you don't have to figure it out on your own as I did. This book is going to be the kick in the pants you need to make you realize that **now is the time to start talking to your parents about their finances.** It will help you get past any fears you have about bringing up this difficult topic. It offers a variety of ways to start the conversation.

It provides encouraging stories from people who've had money talks with their parents. And it's chock-full of advice from financial, legal, and eldercare experts who've helped thousands and thousands of clients navigate family money talks.

To be clear, this book is not geared just toward wealthy families who want to avoid fights over their parents' assets if they die without estate plans. In fact, it's even more important for middle- and lower-income families to be having these conversations as soon as possible to make sure their parents' money doesn't run out in retirement and to have a fallback plan if it does. It's for people who want to find out if their parents know how they're going to pay for any long-term care they might need, because Medicare typically doesn't cover assisted-living costs, and it can be tough to qualify for Medicaid. It's for people who need to know the ins and outs of their parents' finances because they might have to help manage them someday as I did – and still do – for my mom.

I recognize that all families are different and that, no matter how hard you try, your parents might refuse to talk to you about money issues. If you use the strategies I suggest in this book to get your parents to open up but still can't get them to talk, I do offer some practical advice from people who've been in this situation and some tips from experts on how to be prepared for worst-case scenarios. I also recognize that even though I use "parents" throughout the book for simplicity's sake, there is just a single parent in many families – or a mom and mom or dad and dad. In those situations where there is only one parent, it's even more important to have these conversations because there isn't a spouse or partner to provide financial or caregiving support. You, the child, will more likely have to help your parent as he or she ages.

My hope is that you can learn from the mistakes I made – and the things I did right. I want to be a friendly voice – and share the voices of others – to help guide you through the process of talking to your parents about what can be an uncomfortable topic. Most importantly, I want you and your parents to be able to say, "I'm glad we talked."

1

Get Over Your Fear of Having "The Talk"

Do you remember the birds-and-bees talk your parents gave you when you were a kid? It's probably one of those conversations you've tried to repress because it was so awkward. Or perhaps your parents never even bothered to have "the talk" with you.

I remember what happened when I asked my mom where babies came from. She answered that a man and woman lie together and "make love." I'm not kidding – that's all she said. She didn't even follow up with one of those books that parents give their kids when they're too uncomfortable explaining how sex works.

If grades were given for this parental duty, my mom would've gotten a D at best. I have three kids now, so, clearly, I figured out how babies are made – no thanks to my mom, though. But as a mother myself, I recognize how awkward the conversation can be and why plenty of parents try to dodge it.

So what does this have to do with talking to your parents about their finances? A lot.

Sex and money are two of the most taboo topics. However, many people seem to be even more uncomfortable talking about money. A 2016 survey by Care.com[1] found that more than half of parents would rather have the sex talk with their kids than talk to their parents about money and aging issues.

A survey by personal finance website GOBankingRates found that 10 percent of Americans are more comfortable talking about their romantic life with their parents than their parents' finances. And 9 percent said they'd rather talk to their parents about their *parents'* romantic life than ask them about their finances. Who are these people? I totally understand that asking your parents to share details about their finances can be awkward. But I think it would be a lot weirder asking your mom or dad for details about their love life.

Sadly, though, when it comes to having money talks with their parents, many people appear to be taking the approach my mom used for the birds-and-bees talk. They're avoiding the conversation. The GOBankingRates' survey found that 73 percent of adults haven't had detailed conversations with their parents about their finances. One of the most common reasons respondents gave for not having a money talk with their parents is because they're afraid to bring up the topic.

So what is it about this conversation that seems so intimidating? Here is just a small sample of what people have said about why they are afraid to ask their parents about whether they have enough money to support themselves in retirement, who will make financial decisions for them if they no longer can, what happens to their assets when they die, or what their final wishes are.

- "I still find it challenging to speak about money with my parents. We can discuss religion, politics, and relationships, but money remains a taboo subject," Jason said.
- Olivia said she's tried to have conversations with her mom to find out how she will support herself in retirement. But her mom always changes the subject. "I'm kind of afraid to ask more specific questions," Olivia said. "I don't want her to be offended. I don't want her to feel like I'm being nosy."
- "I really don't like those conversations," Noah said about discussing his parents' wills. "I'm really not fond talking about the death of my parents as a potential thing."
- Talking about money with her father has never been easy, Meg said. It's a conversation she knows she needs to have now that he's approaching 70, has unstable finances and long-term health problems, and is in a second marriage. But she's afraid. "Discussing the full scope of

his finances, along with how he and my stepmother have discussed their planning in light of our blended family composition, has been intimidating enough that I've shied away from approaching it with him."

You might share some of these fears, or perhaps you have your own reasons for not wanting to talk to your parents about their finances. But unlike the birds-and-bees talk your parents might have avoided with you, you can't let fear prevent you from having a money talk with your parents. Don't assume you'll just figure out the details of your parents' finances without their input the way you might have figured out how to have your own kids without a sex ed talk from mom or dad. You will be much better prepared for any role you'll have to play in their financial lives as they age if you get a dialogue going.

More importantly, you need to recognize that your fear of how your parents will respond to your questions about their finances is much worse than what will actually happen.

YOUR FEARS VERSUS REALITY

That scenario you've been playing out in your head probably won't materialize. If you have a decent relationship with your parents, you'll find that asking them about their finances won't erupt into a screaming match. In fact, they likely will be grateful that you're looking out for their well-being.

If your relationship with your mom or dad is strained, it might not be quite so easy. But rather than let your fear of what *might* happen if you ask about their finances prevent you from talking to your parents, remember that the reality might not be so bad. At least, that's what the people who shared the following stories discovered.

Fear: My parents will think I'm being nosy.
Reality: They might be glad you asked because they had been meaning to talk with you. Even parents who are reluctant to talk might be grateful, in the long run, that you took the initiative to have a conversation and help them with money issues.

As an accountant, Lisa had always been comfortable talking to people about money. However, it wasn't a conversation she wanted to have with her parents. "You want to make sure they are financially secure but don't want to appear too nosy," she said.

Lisa had to push past that fear, though, when it became obvious that her aging parents were living in a home that was too expensive and difficult for them to maintain. "My siblings and I all wanted them to move to a retirement-type village that would take some of that stress off of them," she said. "Mom was open to the suggestion, but Dad had always owned his own home and thought renting was a terrible idea."

So she sat down with them and their checkbook to total up how much it was costing them to live in their home. Then she prepared a budget showing how much it would cost them to live in a retirement community. "They were shocked how close the numbers were," she said.

But her dad still wasn't willing to move, even though he had been battling prostate cancer for years and his health was going to make it difficult for him to stay in his home. "I had to pull out the big guns to convince him the move was necessary: 'Dad, you'll need a wheelchair soon and these 1929 doorways aren't big enough,'" she said.

"He answered, 'I'm still feeling pretty good. I want to wait until I'm bad,'" Lisa said.

"'If you wait that long, you'll be in nursing care instead of independent living,' I reminded him. 'Then Mom won't be able to be with you,'" she told her dad.

That did the trick. Lisa's father agreed to move. After living in the retirement community for a month, he pulled Lisa aside to tell her thank you. He said he was glad to be in a place where he could look around and *not* see things that needed to be done that he couldn't do anymore.

"Sadly, we lost Dad earlier this year. But because he was in a place where we could roll in the hospital bed and use hospice, he got his wish that his wife and children were at his side," Lisa said. "My best advice to anyone with aging parents is to start the conversation early, before significant life changes are occurring and talk about the 'what ifs.' Dad's stress level would have been greatly reduced had we moved him years before."

Fear: My parents will think I'm being greedy.
Reality: If you make it clear that you're asking about their finances out of concern for their well-being, they will see that you have their best interests at heart – not just yours.

When Becky was in her late 20s, a family friend who had been sick for several years died. Becky started thinking about how the woman and her family had time to prepare for her death and started wondering if her parents, who were in their 60s, had taken any steps to ensure a smooth transition of their assets when they died.

In particular, she wanted to find out whether her father, who is a self-employed musician and writer, had plans for how she and her siblings should handle his business if something happened to him. She was nervous asking this because she recognized it was an uncomfortable topic and didn't want to look like she was just after an inheritance. But she realized that if she didn't initiate the conversation, no one else in her family would.

"I brought it up casually with my parents with my siblings present," Becky said. "They first laughed it off, asking if I planned on getting rid of them."

She wasn't motivated in the least by greed – but rather concern – so she kept at it. "I brought up our family friend and how she was able to plan and prepare," Becky said. "I said that, of course, I wasn't trying to get rid of them, but we – the kids – should know what they both want."

Becky's parents told her and her siblings that they should just let their lawyer and accountant handle the business. But a couple of months later, they told Becky that they had met with their attorney to update their wills to name her executor of their estate. Her parents said that she and her siblings would become board members of their father's company when they died and that their house should be sold and the profit should be split among them. "It was a relief to talk to them about this because I know how families can get once money and real estate is involved," Becky said.

> **Fear: My parents will be offended, and our relationship will be ruined.**
> **Reality: They might like you less in the moment if they're not comfortable with you asking about their finances. But they're your parents. They won't stop loving you. In fact, your relationship might become stronger.**

If you have a good relationship with your parents, you likely don't need to worry about offending them by asking about their finances. Richmond, who is in his 20s, found that having a money talk with his dad wasn't the least bit awkward or uncomfortable. In fact, he said it was a relief to find out that his father was financially prepared for his retirement.

Shortly after his grandfather died in 2015, Richmond sat down with his dad on the porch one night and talked for hours about life, family, and finances. "We talked at length about how their house purchase was a huge stretch, how he prioritized saving for retirement while providing a great quality of life for us kids, and a few things he would have done differently along the way," Richmond said.

Throughout the conversation, Richmond asked questions to get more information. "He was fairly open about the value of their house, the amount inherited from my grandpa, and what his plans for retirement were. I remember asking him specifically when he was going to retire and whether or not he was nervous about it," he said. His father told him that he has saved enough to live comfortably without putting a burden on him or his sisters.

"That moment was incredibly freeing," Richmond said. Since that day, the lines of communication have remained open. And the added benefit has been that Richmond's dad has helped him learn how to manage his own finances, he said.

> **Fear: If my parents resist my efforts to talk, I'll never be able to get them to have a conversation with me about their finances.**

Reality: You might have to try and try again. But your parents may eventually come around and recognize that you're just looking out for them.

When it comes to talking to your parents about their finances, you don't get just one shot. And you certainly don't have to tackle all of their financial issues at one time. In fact, it should be an ongoing conversation, as Whitney discovered.

When Whitney was having financial troubles in her marriage, her mother added her to her bank account so Whitney would have access to money if the going got really tough for her. After a divorce and a new marriage, Whitney got back on track financially. But her mother started having her own financial problems.

Whitney's father had died, so her mom had lost her father's Social Security income. But her mom continued to spend like she had two incomes, Whitney said. At one point, she checked her mom's bank account to make sure everything was okay. The balance was $0.

When she texted her mom to see if she needed money, Whitney's mom texted back, "What are you talking about?" Whitney then called to let her mom know that she had no money in her account.

"She was horribly embarrassed and didn't want to talk about it," Whitney said. But Whitney persisted, and it opened the door to conversations about how much money her mom had coming in and how she was spending her money. She talked to her mom about how to distinguish between her needs and wants. And they went through all of her mom's expenses and figured out what could be trimmed.

"It was a humbling experience for her to go through," Whitney said. "Fortunately, she didn't fight me. She was amenable to the conversation and was, quite frankly, thankful. I don't think she realized how she was spending her money."

Fear: I don't know enough about this to even try.
Truth: This book will get you started.

People have to go through years of coursework and training, pass exams, and get the proper certification to become financial professionals and help others with their money. So how are you – the average person just trying to make sense of your own finances – supposed to start talking to your mom or dad about whether they've taken all of the necessary steps to get their finances in order? You might not even know where to begin or what to ask. Just thinking about financial stuff makes you break out in a sweat. So the idea of having a money talk with your parents is enough to bring on a full-blown panic attack.

Relax. Take a deep breath. That's why I wrote this book. You don't have to be a financial pro to talk to your mom or dad about money matters. I walk you through what to say and what not to say. I explain reasons your parents might be reluctant to discuss their finances with you so you can identify the best approach to take to start a conversation. Then I give you a variety of conversation starters so you can choose the one that works best for your situation.

You'll get tips on talking to your siblings so you can get on the same page and avoid fights over handling your parents' finances down the road. You will find out in great detail what information you need to gather from your parents. Plus, you'll learn the importance of legal documents such as wills, power of attorney, and advance health care directives – in a language you can understand.

You will find out how to broach tough topics such as long-term care. You'll also get strategies to help you get your parents to open up if they're reluctant to share details about their finances with you. And you'll find tips on what to do if your parents absolutely won't talk.

The aim is to make you comfortable and confident enough to have productive conversations with your parents that will benefit both them and you. And, honestly, it's not nearly as awkward as the birds-and-bees conversation. At least you won't leave the conversation thinking, "I did not need *that* image in my head."

Exercise

Write your top fears about talking about your parents. Get them out of your head and onto paper. Your fears could be similar to the ones listed in this chapter, or they could be unique to your own experiences with your parents.

Consider what the chances are that your fears of how your parents will respond when you ask about their finances will actually become reality. Rate your fear on a scale of 1 to 10, with 10 being most likely to happen. Then write at least one reason your fear might *not* become reality.

For example, you might be afraid that your relationship with your parents will be damaged if you ask about their finances because money has always been a taboo topic in your family. You rate this fear a 5. But when you write that you've had a good relationship with your parents, you realize that your parents might be uncomfortable with the topic but not so angry that they'll stop talking to you altogether.

This exercise will help you assess how valid your fear is and, hopefully, will help you realize that a conversation will likely go better than you think.

NOTE

1. Katie Bugbee (2017), "How Senior Care Impacts Families Financially, Emotionally and in the Workplace," https://www.care.com/c/stories/7303/how-senior-care-impacts-families-financially/ (Accessed Jan. 2, 2019).

CHAPTER 2

Don't Wait

One of the biggest mistakes you can make when it comes to talking to your parents about their finances is assuming that the conversation can wait. You might be telling yourself, "I'll cross that bridge when I come to it ... when they're having health problems or their finances are an issue." At that point, it might be too late.

I made that mistake with my mom and still regret it. As I wrote in the introduction, my mom was 65 when she was diagnosed with Alzheimer's disease, and I was 35. I never expected that I would have to start taking care of my mom while I still had kids in diapers. In fact, I assumed that my mom would be able to help me with my children.

Even as she was starting to show signs of memory loss, I hung onto to the idea that my mom would be there for me and my kids. So I wasn't in any rush to discuss the "what ifs" with her: *What if you start having trouble keeping track of your finances? What if I have to manage your money for you? What if you have to move into an assisted living facility or nursing home?*

I didn't want to talk about money matters because it meant confronting the fact that she was losing her memory. I delayed the conversation until it became apparent that I couldn't put it off any longer. Then I had to scramble.

I had to make sure I had the legal right to help make financial and health care decisions for her. That meant meeting with an attorney to draft power of attorney and living will documents. Fortunately, as my mom's memory was starting to falter, the attorney still deemed her competent enough to give me power of attorney. For power of attorney to be valid, you have to be mentally competent when you sign it. If I had waited any longer than I did to encourage her to see an attorney to update her estate planning documents, she might not have been found fit to sign them.

Without power of attorney, I wouldn't have been able to manage my mom's money for her once she no longer could. Her bank, investment firms, credit card companies, and insurance companies wouldn't have let me make any financial transactions for her. Instead, I would have needed to go through the court system to be appointed her conservator. That can be a lengthy and expensive process, and you have to prove – with a diagnosis from a doctor – that your parent is incompetent.

Getting power of attorney was actually a lot easier than the detective work I did after that to figure out what financial accounts and sources of income my mom had and what bills needed to be paid. If I had had the wherewithal to talk with my mom about her finances well before her health declined, I would've avoided a lot of the panic and stress I felt (and she probably felt, too). But like many people, I assumed that the conversation could wait.

A survey by Fidelity Investments[1] found that nearly 40 percent of adult children think conversations about their parents' finances don't need to happen until *after* their parents have retired and their health or finances have become an issue. Another 11 percent think discussions don't need to happen until their parents are retiring.

This wait-and-see approach is entirely understandable. Many of us are so busy with our daily lives that we don't stop to think about taking the time to talk to our parents about their financial lives.

We assume there will be time for that later. We might also think our parents have a handle on their finances and a plan for worst-case scenarios, so there's no need to talk. Or we might assume that Mom or Dad will come to us if they need help.

Wrong, wrong, and wrong.

I know I sound like the bossy kid on the playground saying that. But I'm speaking from personal experience – and with the wisdom of a financial journalist who has read countless surveys and studies on these issues. The reality is that your parents might not have a good handle on money matters. They probably won't initiate a conversation about their finances or ask for help if they need it. And, most importantly, time really is not on your side.

YOUR PARENTS MIGHT NOT HAVE THEIR FINANCIAL ACT TOGETHER

Let me let you in on a little secret: There's a good chance your parents aren't on top of their finances. How do I know this? Because many adults aren't making all of the right financial moves and haven't taken the steps to prepare for retirement, for long-term care needs, or even for their death. Consider these statistics:

- A Gallup poll[2] found that nearly half of adults ages 50 to 64 **don't have a will**, and more than one-third of adults 65 and older don't have a will.
- An AARP study[3] found that 55 percent of adults over 50 **don't have a durable power of attorney** – someone who is legally appointed to make financial decisions for them if they can't.
- Nearly half of adults **don't have a health care power of attorney** who is designated to make medical decisions for them if they can't, a Caring.com survey[4] found.
- A survey by the Insured Retirement Institute[5] found that 45 percent of baby boomers ages 53 to 69 **don't have money saved for retirement**.
- Only 27 percent of boomers think they have enough money for **health care expenses** in retirement, the IRI survey found.
- Just 5 percent of adults ages 55 to 60 have **long-term care insurance**, and only 11 percent of adults 65 and older have a policy, according to the Urban Institute.[6]

You might be thinking, "Maybe my parents don't have a will or estate planning documents, ample retirement savings, or an insurance policy that will help pay for long-term care. So what?"

Here's what:

Your own finances could take a big hit if your parents need support from you in retirement, or if you have to stop working to care for a parent who needs long-term care. Medicaid pays for care in nursing homes and at home, but you have to meet income and other requirements. Medicare typically doesn't cover long-term care in an assisted living facility or a nursing home – but long-term-care insurance does.

You or your siblings might not have the legal authority to step in and make financial or health care decisions for your parents if they haven't given you power of attorney or health care power of attorney. If an accident or illness leaves your dad or mom mentally incompetent, he or she won't be able to sign these legal documents.

Family fights could erupt and long, expensive court battles could ensue if your parents die without a will specifying who gets what. It might not go that far, but it certainly can create tension and resentment.

These are just a handful of ways you could be impacted if your parents don't have their financial act together. Are you starting to see why having a money talk with your parents can't wait? No? Okay, I'll keep going.

YOUR PARENTS PROBABLY WON'T INITIATE A CONVERSATION

Money might not seem like a taboo topic to you, but it likely is for your parents' generation. Less than half of baby boomers surveyed by Ameriprise Financial[7] – and even fewer of their parents – said they grew up in a household where money was discussed openly. So many older adults may still be hanging onto the idea that their finances are private. As a result, they're not going to stop by for a visit or give you a call to say, "Hey kids, let's have a heart-to-heart about our financial situation today."

There are plenty of other reasons your parents might not initiate a conversation with you about their finances – which I discuss in more detail in Chapter 3. They might be embarrassed that they're not on top of their finances. They might feel like they're burdening you by bringing up money issues. Or it's just not something that's at the top of their minds.

The Ameriprise survey found that among baby boomers who haven't talked to their kids about their finances, the most common reasons they gave were "haven't gotten around to it" and "haven't thought about it." If you're a boomer, those might also be reasons why your parents haven't talked to *you* about their finances, either.

But here's where it gets interesting. Even though your parents might not initiate a conversation with you about their finances, there's a good chance they are counting on your help as they age. A Fidelity Investments' Family & Finance Study[8] found that parents aren't making their wishes heard:

- 69 percent of parents expect one of their children to help manage their finances in retirement, but more than one-third of children who are expected to fill this role didn't know this.
- 72 percent of parents expect one of their children to be their caregiver if necessary, but 40 percent of children identified as filling this role didn't know this.
- 92 percent of parents expect one of their children to be the executor of their estate when they die, but more than a quarter of kids who are expected to fill this role didn't know this.

Don't you want to know if you're parents are expecting you to play an active role in their financial lives or help care for them? Wouldn't you rather know *now* than right at the moment you actually have to step in and help?

IT'S NEVER TOO EARLY TO TALK

Sometimes even parents you would expect to be totally on top of all aspects of their finances might not be. Case in point: My dad was an attorney, but he died without a will at the age of 61. I assumed that because he drafted wills for other people as part of his job, he would have had that base covered. But I never asked, and he never brought up topics like death or money.

When I got married a year before his death, I would've had a great opportunity to get a conversation going with my dad. I could have asked him for his advice about whether I needed a will or any other legal documents now that I was married. And that could have led to a discussion about what he had in place.

But I didn't realize it was a conversation I needed to have. If I had, it might have prevented the awkward situation my sister and I were thrown into after his death. My parents had divorced many years earlier, and my dad had remarried. Because he died without a will, we'll never know how he wanted his assets divided among me, my sister, my stepmom and stepbrother, or any other family members.

I now have several of my dad's belongings – including his antique roll-top desk that I'm sitting at to write this book – thanks to my wonderful stepbrother, who made sure I got them after his mother died at the age of 64 after a battle with cancer. But it's not always so civil when parents die without a will, especially if they've remarried or there are children from more than one marriage. In the grand scheme of things, I consider myself lucky because it could've turned out worse.

Nonetheless, the awkwardness that arose after my dad died without a will might have been avoided entirely if I had recognized the importance of talking to him about money matters and estate planning. But like many people, I wasn't in a rush to have the conversation.

My experience shows that the wait-and-see approach isn't a good one. You're probably thinking that the chances are pretty slim that you'll end up in a situation like I did with one parent dying at a relatively young age without a will and another diagnosed with Alzheimer's at age 65. I could spout off more statistics to prove that the odds are higher than you might think. But you might be more convinced just by considering all of the people you know who've already been thrown into a situation where they have to get involved with their parents' finances – as a result of illness, dementia, a debilitating accident, death, or just poor money management.

I know it's hard to think about our parents getting older or dying. Your parents might have taught you to stash spare change in a piggy bank when you were a kid. But you might have to make sure their bank accounts aren't drained by scammers who take advantage of them as they age. Your parents made sure you had food, clothing, and a roof over your head. You may have to ensure that they have the same in retirement if their Social Security benefits and savings aren't enough to live comfortably. They took care of you, and you might have to do the same for them someday.

Having a money talk with your parents can bring all of those uncomfortable scenarios to the forefront. But the sooner you start having conversations with your parents, the better. Here's why:

- You and your parents will have more time to come up with a plan if it looks like they won't have enough money to live comfortably in retirement.
- You and your parents will have more time to discuss what sort of care they want if an illness or accident leaves them unable to take care of themselves and how to pay for that care.
- You and your parents will have time to discuss what roles they want you to play – such as power of attorney or execu-tor of their estate – then get legal documents drafted and signed.

Most importantly, talking to your parents sooner rather than later will give you peace of mind. Then you can *spend the time you do have* with your parents without that nagging feeling that you're not prepared to give them the help they might some-day need.

NOTES

1. Fidelity Investments (2016), "2016 Fidelity Investments Family & Finance Study Executive Summary," https://www.fidelity.com/bin-public/060_www _fidelity_com/documents/Family-Finance-Study-Executive-Summary.pdf (Accessed Jan. 2, 2019).
2. Gallup, Jeffrey M. Jones (2016), "Majority in U.S. Do Not Have a Will," https://news.gallup.com/poll/191651/majority-not.aspx (Accessed Jan. 2, 2019).
3. AARP (2000), "Where There Is a Will ... Legal Documents Among the 50+ Population: Findings from an AARP Survey," https://assets.aarp.org/rgcenter/econ/will.pdf (Accessed Jan. 2, 2019).
4. Caring.com, "Estate Planning by the Numbers," https://www.caring.com/articles/estate-planning-by-the-numbers-infographic (Accessed Jan. 2, 2019).
5. Insured Retirement Institute (2016), "Boomer Expectations for Retirement 2016," https://www.myirionline.org/docs/default-source/research/boomer-expectations-for-retirement-2016.pdf?sfvrsn=2 (Accessed Jan. 2, 2019).
6. Urban Institute, Richard W. Johnson (2016), "Who Is Covered by Private Long-Term Care Insurance?" https://www.urban.org/research/publication/who-covered-private-long-term-care-insurance (Accessed Jan. 2, 2019).
7. Ameriprise Financial (2007), "Ameriprise Financial Money Across Generations Survey Reveals Finances Still a Taboo Topic at the Family Dinner Table," https://www.businesswire.com/news/home/20071115006123/en/Ameriprise-Financial-Money-Generations-SM-Study-Reveals (Accessed Jan. 2, 2019).
8. Fidelity Investments (2016), "Fidelity Investments Family & Finance Study Executive Summary," https://www.fidelity.com/bin-public/060_www _fidelity_com/documents/Family-Finance-Study-Executive-Summary.pdf (Accessed Jan. 2, 2019).

3

Reasons Your Parents Might Be Reluctant to Talk

Amanda knows she needs to start talking to her parents about their finances but is reluctant to have the conversation. They've been hard workers most of their lives but haven't been high earners. Her mom stayed at home with her and her two sisters until they started school. She then had jobs at McDonald's and Blake's Lotaburger while going to school herself to become a paralegal. She worked for the same attorney as a paralegal for 25 years until 2017, when his health issues forced him to downsize his practice and he let her go. Since then, she's been helping care for her elderly mother, her husband's father, and her niece's young children, and she's been doing some side work for another attorney.

Amanda's dad has worked in a variety of jobs, including a correctional officer at a prison and a lab worker in a refinery. Currently, he works with a county property assessor's office but might lose his job because the county is facing bankruptcy.

"Although my parents have always been frugal and have been careful with money, they are at a place where they are really feeling anxious about their finances," Amanda said. "They have a private retirement account, and my dad should have some retirement benefits through his employment. However, I honestly have no idea how much they have. My parents do not like to share their financial information with us."

In fact, Amanda's parents taught her and her sisters as they were growing up that talking about finances is taboo. They trained them to avoid questions about money by changing the subject. Given her parents' current situation, Amanda said she is concerned about their financial future. But she knows they'll be reluctant to talk to her.

John remembers that, when he was growing up, his parents never talked about money. If it came up during a conversation, they would find a way to change the subject. Or they would "talk about how they always got screwed in some way with money," he said.

Like many people in their generation, John's parents were taught not to talk about money. They held onto that belief and refused to discuss financial matters with John and his sisters when they were young. Money conversations didn't get any easier as the kids got older. But it wasn't just because John's parents believed that that money was a taboo topic. John said the real reason his parents have avoided talking about money over the years is because they have been ashamed of how they've mismanaged it.

When John was young, his parents made a lot of money. But they spent even more, he said. So they struggled financially. Their overspending was so bad that they raided John's bank account when he was 17 and took every penny he had saved for college because they claimed they needed help paying bills.

John's parents are now divorced and still are struggling financially, he said. His father has been unemployed for more than 10 years and has been living with one of John's sisters. His mom still works and likely will have to as long as she can because she can't afford to retire. John – who is a successful entrepreneur – has tried to help them get a better handle on their finances. But he said their shame and pride have gotten in the way of having fruitful conversations.

Some parents will openly discuss their finances with their adult children, but plenty – like Amanda's and John's parents – will balk at the conversation. However, knowing what might be behind your parents' unwillingness to talk might help you identify the best way to start a conversation. Why? Think of it as putting yourself in their shoes – an expression you likely heard from your parents throughout your childhood. If you can imagine thinking about money the way your parents do, you can approach the topic in a way that won't make them uncomfortable or put them on the defensive.

So how do you actually do that? Start by determining whether any of these common reasons older adults can be reluctant to talk about money apply to your parents.

THEY THINK MONEY IS A TABOO TOPIC

Think back to your childhood. Did your parents typically tell you it's not polite to talk about money? Maybe that was the response you got when you asked how much they earned, how much the family car cost, or whether your family was rich or poor.

It's common for older generations to shy away from the topic of money because they've been taught it is taboo, said Dr. Brad Klontz,[1] a financial psychologist. "Parents would rather talk to their kids about sex than money," he said. So if you remember that asking Mom and Dad money questions made them even more uncomfortable than asking about the birds and the bees, recognize that they're likely clinging to a deep-seated conviction that conversations about money are off-limits.

If that's the case, **don't make your initial attempts at having financial conversations with your parents about money**. In Chapter 7, I provide some conversation starters that don't involve tackling the topic of money head on but can get your parents to open up about their finances over time.

THEY DON'T WANT ROLES TO BE REVERSED

Parents have a strong instinct to care for their children. That instinct doesn't disappear once their children are grown. So it can feel like the tables are being turned on them when their kids want to talk about how to care for them or help them with financial matters, said Dr. Mary Gresham,[2] a financial psychologist. "That's a place that goes against the grain," she said.

Parents don't want to have to think about having to depend on their children. So that's why they might balk at conversations that force them to consider this scenario. But if you can frame the reversal of care in positive terms, you might have more luck getting them to talk.

When initiating a conversation, **let your parents know that you're grateful that they took care of you when you were young and that you want to be able to return that care if they need it**. You can tell them that in order to do that, you need to know what sort of care they would want. Let them know that you realize this might be difficult for them to think about or discuss. Gresham recommends saying something like, "I know this is a hard conversation. It's upsetting to me, too, but I still want to have it. Think of it as a gift to me."

THEY FEAR THE CONVERSATION WILL UPSET YOU

Your parents might be dodging conversations about their finances because they're afraid you won't like what they have to say. This could likely be the case if you've been trying to talk to them about their wills and estate plans, and they've consistently balked at discussing this topic.

Parents are often secretive about what's in their wills because they're worried their kids will get mad if they find out they're not inheriting as much as they think, Gresham said. Your parents might be planning to leave their money to a charity. Or they might be planning to give more to one of your siblings – perhaps because they feel he needs more financial support than you do. But they don't want you to know because they're afraid it will hurt your relationship with them.

Gresham said she's had clients who've said they know that the way they've planned to distribute assets among their kids when they die could put a strain on the relationships between siblings. They avoid telling their kids what's in their wills so fights won't erupt while they're still living. They say that once they die and the kids find out who gets what, they won't have to deal with the fallout. Talk about kicking the can down the road. But it's understandable that they want to avoid confrontation.

If you suspect that your parents are avoiding money conversations because they don't want to upset you, **let them know that**

you think your relationship with them – and your siblings – is strong enough to talk freely. And tell them you realize it's their money and they can do with it what they want but it would be great to have some insight into their plans so there aren't surprises.

Or keep money out of the conversation. Let your parents know that you're not interested in how much you will inherit, Klontz said. Instead, tell them, "We just want to make sure we're clear on what your wishes are with your estate." Show them that you want to make sure that those wishes are granted. See Chapter 10 to learn more about essential legal documents.

THEY'RE WORRIED ABOUT LOSING THEIR INDEPENDENCE

Remember when you started driving? You could go where you wanted when you wanted. You had freedom. You had independence. Or perhaps it was when you got your first job and had your own money that you started to feel independent. Maybe it was when you graduated from college and entered the real world.

Being independent is a great feeling, and wanting to be autonomous is a deep human drive, Gresham said. So if you start talking to your parents about their future, it's natural for them to be reluctant to think about and discuss a time when they might no longer be independent. Planning for a time when they can't do things on their own represents a huge loss of status. They could be thinking, "When I give you this information, I could lose control," Gresham said.

That's why it's so important to **make it clear to your parents when talking to them about their finances that you don't want to take control and deprive them of their independence**. Let them stay in charge by asking them to make a list of potential situations in which they would need support from you and what would need to happen. You could tell them you're giving them control because they're deciding if and when you should step in – and to what extent. However, if your parents already are at the point where they need assistance with day-to-day living and are no longer capable of living independently, see Chapters 12 and 13 for tips on talking to them about long-term care and when it's time to move.

THEY'RE EMBARRASSED ABOUT THEIR FINANCES

Like John's parents, your parents might be ashamed about the state of their finances. Maybe they're deep in debt, have no savings, are living paycheck to paycheck, or have no idea how they'll ever be able to afford to retire. So talking to you about money means admitting that they've done things wrong – something they probably don't want to do.

They're probably afraid that you'll judge them or criticize them for not having their financial act together. Shame often prevents people from talking openly about money. So if you suspect that your parents are embarrassed about their financial situation, you'll need to tread lightly.

Gresham recommends trying this approach: "I understand you're avoiding this topic with me. I've brought it up three or four times. I want to understand your reluctance. Are you concerned I might judge you if you don't have it all organized? Are you concerned I might look at you differently if you don't have as much as I think?" **Reassure your parents that you won't judge them and that you just want to help.** I provide more details on getting through to reluctant parents in Chapter 14 and share stories in Chapter 15 from people who've been able to get parents who are embarrassed about their finances to open up to them.

THEY DON'T WANT TO THINK ABOUT AGING AND DEATH

In Chapter 1, I included a quote from Noah, who said he was afraid to talk to his parents about whether they had a will because it meant facing the fact that they will die someday. Your parents might be avoiding your attempts to talk about estate planning, long-term care, or their financial future for the same reason. It forces them to think about aging and death.

Some people even think that talking about their death will make it happen sooner rather than later. You probably already know if your parents fall into this category because they say things like, "We don't talk about that in our house" or "When your father dies, God forbid ..." as if some higher power will prevent him from dying. An estate law attorney I know said that she often hears from clients that they're afraid they'll die once she drafts an estate plan for them. She then jokes with them that she doesn't have that kind of power.

In all seriousness, though, death can be a scary topic for a lot of people. **Respect that your parents could be afraid of confronting their mortality.** But have the courage to tell them – in a caring, not mocking, way – that having conversations about whether they have a will or what their final wishes are won't hasten their death. In fact, Gresham said that research shows that the more people are aware of and able to talk about their death, the better they'll be able to come to terms with it and feel less anxious about their future.

THEY DON'T TRUST YOU

I hate to say this, but your parents might not want to talk to you about their finances because they don't trust you. You might not have given them any reason to question your intentions. It's just tough, in general, to trust someone else with financial information. As people age, they tend to become even more mistrustful.

Gresham said that when her mother was still alive, she took her to Blockbuster to open an account so she could rent videos. A store employee asked Gresham's mom for her Social Security number as part of the registration process. "She got really upset and said she'd never share it 'with the likes of you,'" Gresham said. "She lost her temper and left."

Fear of being taken advantage of is common among older adults – and for good reason. Research by True Link Financial[3] found that seniors lose $36.5 billion a year to elder financial abuse in the form of scams, misleading financial advice, and theft by family members or caregivers. If your parents are mistrustful, ask them under what circumstances they would feel more comfortable talking to you about their finances. They might be more willing to have a conversation with their accountant, attorney, financial planner, or other third party present.

However, your parents might not want to speak with you about their finances under any circumstances if you've given them reason to believe they can't trust you. Perhaps you've mismanaged your own finances or borrowed money from them and never repaid it. In that case, **you might not be the best person to have a money talk with your parents**. If you have a sibling your parent is more likely to trust, ask him or her to initiate the conversation. Chapter 5 has tips on talking to your siblings about money conversations with your parents.

Exercise

If your parents tend to avoid conversations about money, make a list of the possible reasons why they don't want to talk about this topic. Recognizing what might be behind your parents' unwillingness to discuss financial matters can help you empathize with them. It also will help you identify which conversation starter in Chapter 7 might be the most likely to work.

NOTES

1. Dr. Brad Klontz, https://www.yourmentalwealth.com/about-us/dr-brad-klontz/ (Accessed Jan. 3, 2019).
2. Dr. Mary Gresham, http://doctorgresham.com/ (Accessed Jan. 3, 2019).
3. True Link Financial (2015), "The True Link Report on Elder Financial Abuse 2015," http://documents.truelinkfinancial.com/True-Link-Report-On-Elder-Financial-Abuse-012815.pdf (Accessed Jan. 2, 2019).

4

What Happens If You Don't Have the Conversation

When it comes to talking to your parents about their finances, you might be telling yourself ...

> *I'll wait until they're retired.*
> *I'll wait until health problems make it necessary to have a conversation.*
> *I'll wait until they can no longer take care of themselves.*

If you keep waiting, it will be too late. Your parents might not be mentally capable of sharing details of their finances with you. They might end up in the hospital with health issues, but the doctors won't let you make any medical decisions for them because they didn't designate you as their health care power of attorney. They might die without wills, and you and other family members might end up in court duking it out over who gets what.

One of my biggest regrets is not talking to my mom sooner about the details of her finances – before Alzheimer's disease started robbing her of her memory. Other people I know who've had to step in and help their parents when a crisis struck have said they wish they had acted sooner to ensure their parents had essential legal documents drafted, to get a list of their financial accounts and to make plans for worst-case scenarios. It's so much harder to be reactive than proactive – especially because emotions and the stress of a crisis situation can get in the way of a rational response.

Plus, it can be a whole lot more expensive. Just ask Doug Nordman. He could have avoided spending tens of thousands of dollars – and countless hours of legal proceedings – if he had gotten details about his dad's finances sooner. Doug's story is just one example of the many financial disasters that could happen if you don't have money talks with your parents.

DOUG'S STORY

Doug Nordman[1] is savvy with money – savvy enough to have retired at the age of 41 after 20 years of service with the U.S. Navy submarine force. He writes a popular blog that helps other military members achieve financial independence. Doug has even published a book that shows veterans how to retire on their own terms.

Yet, as comfortable as he has been doling out financial advice to others, Doug was reluctant to discuss money matters with his dad – even when he could see that dementia was hurting his dad's ability to manage his finances. His father, Dean, started showing signs of dementia in 2008. By 2009, his symptoms had worsened, and he wrote to Doug and his brother that his slipping memory had made it hard for him to use the computer. For that reason, he was no longer going to email them and wanted to let them know that he'd be writing them letters instead.

"That earned him a visit from the two of us right away," Doug said. His father was a widower and lived alone in an apartment in Grand Junction, Colorado. When Doug flew from his home in Hawaii and his brother came from Denver, they could see that their dad was showing symptoms of early-stage Alzheimer's disease. He had memos to himself posted around the apartment. The food in his refrigerator had been labeled for each day of the week so he would know when to eat it. When he made meals, he had to search through most of his cupboards before finding a plate. He couldn't remember anything short term.

"I remember thinking this dementia might be caused by his blood pressure medication," Doug said. "I remember thinking,

'This is a problem, and he's going to go to the doctor. He's going to get his blood pressure medication fixed and things will get better.'"

But Doug was worried enough to ask his dad if he needed help. "I remember having a conversation with him. 'Dad, if you want any help with anything, I'm happy to help. If you want me to help you with your bills, I can help you with that. If you want me to help you with your checking account, I can help balance your checkbook. If you want me to help you if you want to get power of attorney, I can help with that. Whatever you want.'"

His dad didn't want help. So Doug told his dad to call if he ever needed anything. "At the time, I didn't feel comfortable pushing," he said. "Believe me, I was ignorant."

Doug said now he realizes that his dad rejected his offer because one of the easiest things for people who have dementia or are cognitively impaired find to say is the word no. "It's not that they're paranoid," he said. "It's not that they're suspicious that you'll take all of their money and scam them. It's just that the default answer is, 'No, I don't think I want to do that.'"

Doug's dad never did call to ask for help – even as his Alzheimer's left him unable to drive and made it harder to cope on his own. However, Doug did get a call in 2011 at 3 a.m. from an emergency room surgeon. His dad had been taken to the hospital because he was in a lot of pain. A CT scan found that he had a bleeding ulcer, and the surgeon had to repair the leak.

Doug said that the first question the surgeon asked when he called was whether his dad had a drinking problem. The doctor said when they opened his abdominal cavity, it was awash in alcohol. Turns out, Doug's dad had been having a drink in the afternoons, then another and another – forgetting how many he'd already had. "He had been consuming at least a pint of scotch a day for several months," Doug said. And he wasn't eating much. "That alcohol with no food burned an ulcer in his stomach."

Doug hopped on a flight from Hawaii to Colorado. When he got there, he and his brother had to scramble to find a nursing facility where their dad could stay for rehabilitation after his surgery. Doug knew, though, that his dad wouldn't be able to live on his own anymore. So he had to figure out what to do with his dad's apartment – and his finances, which is where he ran into real problems.

Doug wanted to make sure his dad's bills were being paid while he was recovering from his surgery. So he filled out checks and had his dad sign them. However, his dad's handwriting was shaky, so his signature didn't look like his own. This sent up a red flag at his father's bank. The bank manager said the checks could've been forged. Doug explained that his father had been in the hospital and he was helping him pay the bills. Although Doug was acting in his dad's best interest, the bank manager was worried about elder abuse. "She said, 'Before I give you any more access to your father's accounts, I'm going to have to have power of attorney,'" Doug said.

A power of attorney document lets you designate someone to make financial decisions and transactions for you. (I explain it in detail in Chapter 10.) However, you have to be mentally competent when you sign a power of attorney document for it to be valid. Doug's dad, Dean, hadn't given either of his sons power of attorney. Now that he had Alzheimer's, it was too late. When Doug told the bank manager that he couldn't get power of attorney for his dad, she said he would have to apply for conservatorship.

Like a power of attorney, a conservator has legal authority to manage someone's financial affairs. But the process of becoming a conservator can be lengthy and expensive – as Doug discovered.

You have to petition the court to become a conservator, so Doug hired an attorney to file the legal documents and represent him. He also hired an attorney to represent his father, whom he had to prove wasn't capable of making financial decisions on his own. "My dad was the defendant," Doug said. "He was being accused of being incompetent and not being able to manage his affairs."

To prove he was mentally incompetent, Doug had his father evaluated by a neuropsychiatrist – which cost $3,670. Doug also had to prove to the court that he was capable and responsible enough to manage his father's finances for him. He had to pass a credit check, a background check, and a criminal check, and be interviewed by a court-appointed investigator – who grilled Doug about his qualifications to manage his dad's finances and wasn't convinced that he was capable until Doug mentioned that he'd written a book about money. "He said, 'You wrote a book.' Suddenly, I was totally credible because I'd published a book on military personal finance," Doug said.

The entire process of hiring attorneys, petitioning the court to become a conservator, and going through the legal proceedings took nine months, Doug said. And it cost $10,000.

During that time, his dad was receiving a pension and Social Security benefits, but Doug couldn't touch the money to pay for his dad's care because he didn't have legal authority. So he paid $25,000 out of his own pocket to pay the bills. Eventually, Doug was able to reimburse himself from his dad's funds after he became conservator and the court approved the reimbursement. But it would've been a huge financial strain for Doug if he didn't have savings of his own. "I can't imagine doing this if I didn't have my own financial act together," he said. "You can't just go out and spend $25,000 for a medical emergency."

Doug's dad remained at the nursing facility where he went for rehab after his surgery as an Alzheimer's patient. (He eventually moved to a memory-care facility in 2016.) And Doug took over his dad's finances – which was no easy task. "If parents don't talk with their kids, as many don't, you have to do forensic accounting," he said. "You go into their house, have to toss all their file cabinets looking for any hint on what accounts they have, where the money is and passwords – my gosh, passwords." Doug got lucky because he found a list of his dad's accounts and passwords in a drawer. Dean had a will, an advance health care directive that spelled out the end-of-life care he wanted, sizable retirement savings, and a long-term-care insurance policy with coverage worth $318,000.

The long-term care policy helped pay the $6,000 monthly fee for Dean's assisted living, but Doug had to spend a few hours each week filling out and sending paperwork to the insurer to get reimbursed for the cost of care. He also had to track every dollar he spent of his father's money. As conservator, Doug had to file annual reports of his dad's assets and expenses with the court. "If you're not trained in the ability to track finances and prepare a written report, it's a challenge," Doug said. It's something he wouldn't have had to do if he had talked to his dad before he developed dementia and his dad had given him power of attorney. But he did it for six years until his father died in November 2017.

Doug said that if he and his brother had lived closer to their dad, they would've noticed his symptoms of dementia sooner. "Maybe back then we could've had a conversation. 'Hey, Dad, I don't want to manage your stuff, but you need to get a power of attorney and hold onto it until you need it.' Or, 'Let's set up a separate checking account with the two of us jointly. You kick in $1,000, and that way I have the money to help you if you ever need help.' If we'd had that conversation before 2009 when he told us he couldn't use a computer any more, maybe we could've gotten a power of attorney and all of this could have been handled. But by the time it came around to 2009, it was too late. He was already in the mode of 'no' is the easiest thing to say."

Doug's story shows why it's so important not to put off conversations with your parents – especially conversations about whether they have essential legal documents such as power of attorney and health care power of attorney. If you ask your parents about whether they've named anyone to make financial or health care decisions for them if they are no longer able to and they answer no, take the time to share Doug's story so they recognize the importance of having the legal paperwork to prevent worst-case scenarios.

NOTE

1. Doug Nordman, https://the-military-guide.com/for-the-media/authors-biography/ (Accessed Jan. 3, 2019).

CHAPTER

5

Start by Talking to Your Siblings

Now that you've analyzed the reasons your parents might be reluctant to discuss their finances with you and have gotten over your own fears about having the talk, it's time to roll up your sleeves and get down to the business of having a conversation with Mom or Dad, right? Well, not quite.

Before you start talking to your parents, you need to talk to your siblings.

I know what you're thinking: Why do I need to get them involved? My little brother is too self-absorbed even to care about this sort of thing, and my big sister will try to take over and do everything her way. Talking to my parents about their finances is awkward enough without having to deal with my siblings. Please, can't we just leave them out of it?

No, not if you don't want to create feelings of resentment or spark a family feud. I know this because I've seen what happens when siblings don't get on the same page before talking to their parents about money matters or big financial decisions they need to make. It could go something like this:

Sister No. 1: Hey, I talked to Mom and Dad the other day about their wills and stuff like that. I wanted to make sure they had everything in order.

Sister No. 2: Oh. You mean you talked to them about their wills to make sure you got the most. Of course you would because you're their favorite.

Sister No. 1: No, that's not at all what I was trying to do. I just wanted to talk to them because I have a friend whose dad died recently and it was a big mess because he didn't have a will. His second wife's kids were trying to get all of his money, and they ended up having a big court battle. I certainly don't expect us to fight over Mom and Dad's money after they die, but I wanted to make sure they actually had estate planning documents so there wouldn't be any questions about what they wanted.

Sister No. 2: If that's true, why are you waiting until now to tell me you talked to them? Why didn't you let me know you were going to have this conversation before you talked to Mom and Dad? I guess you think I just don't know enough about this sort of thing and wouldn't care. Well, you're wrong. But, of course, you'd never admit that because you're the oldest and that means you're always right.

Ouch.

A fight won't necessarily erupt if you decide to talk to Mom or Dad before consulting your siblings, especially if you have a good relationship. But you'll be in a much better position to ensure that all of you are acting in your parents' best interest if you've already had discussions, come to a consensus, and developed plans together to deal with worst-case scenarios. My friend Elizabeth wishes she had had conversations with her two older brothers sooner for that reason.

After their dad died, the three of them were butting heads because each had his or her own idea about where their mom should live now that she was alone and in her 80s. Although their mom initially wanted to remain in her house, she decided instead to move to the city where her sons live. Elizabeth's oldest brother didn't want his mom to sell his childhood home, so he didn't play much of a role in helping the other brother search for a new house for their mom, which led to lots of arguments between the two. Elizabeth, on the other hand, thought her mom would be better off in a retirement community, where she would be surrounded by people her age and would not have to worry about maintaining a house.

Elizabeth said she and her brothers should've talked long before their father died to agree on what would be best for their mom once she was on her own. Then they could've approached her as a united front and helped her plan financially – and prepare emotionally – for a living arrangement that would be better suited for her as a widow. Putting off the conversation only led to fighting as they tried to deal with their mom's housing dilemma on the fly. And their mom ended up in a place that was far from ideal – a house with stairs that she'll have trouble climbing. It's in a noisy neighborhood without people her age, so she is isolated. And she can't maintain the property on her own.

Kathy, on the other hand, is a great example of how talking to your siblings before discussing financial matters with your parents can make things so much easier for everyone. Kathy is Kathy Kristof,[1] an award-winning financial journalist who's written three books about personal finance. So you might argue that she has a certain leg up when it comes to discussing money matters. But she credits keeping an open line of communication with her sister, Moira – rather than financial savvy – for creating a game plan to talk to their parents.

Kathy brought up the topic of talking to their parents with her sister after watching her then boyfriend (now husband) deal with the financial fallout from his stepdad's death and his mother's stroke. She told her sister, "We've never talked about this, but we should get documents in order so Mom and Dad can get the best care." By documents, Kathy meant talking to their parents about drafting power of attorney and health care power of attorney documents to designate someone to make financial and medical decisions for them if they couldn't make decisions on their own.

After discussing the matter together several times, they agreed that they would ask their parents to go to an estate planning attorney with them so they all could have legal documents drafted to prepare for worst-case scenarios and could decide what role each person would play. Kathy's parents named her their financial power of attorney and named her sister their health care power of attorney. "We were all making those decisions in public so when the time rolled around, nobody would be surprised," she said.

Having those conversations and planning before a crisis struck paid off because Kathy and her sister had the legal right to step in and help when their mom was diagnosed at age 80 with lung cancer and went through treatment. The effects of the treatment had left their mom unable to think clearly. And their dad didn't feel capable of making decisions, either, because his own health wasn't good. "They needed the next generation to step in and do some of the heavy lifting," Kathy said.

Because she was her mom's health care power of attorney, Moira was able to discuss her mom's treatment options with her doctors and make decisions for her. And Kathy was able to handle the financial side of things, such as insurance paperwork and bills. "To me, having that financial power of attorney and health care advocate – those are the most important things you can talk to your parents about," Kathy said. "Hopefully, your parents feel like they can trust you to stand in their stead to make sure they're getting what they need."

As for her and her sister, Kathy said they work as a team. "When we don't agree, we have conversations that are civil," she said. "We're both after our parents' best interest."

So how do you get past any sibling rivalry and differences of opinion that might exist to have fruitful conversations with your brothers or sisters? And what do you need to agree on with your siblings before sitting down to talk with your parents about their finances, estate planning, and potential long-term care needs?

GET ON THE SAME PAGE WITH YOUR SIBLINGS

I feel fortunate that my sister, Robin, and I haven't had any disputes since I stepped in to help my mom manage her finances after her Alzheimer's diagnosis. We haven't had a particularly close relationship until recently, but that never stopped us from agreeing on my mom's care and how to pay for it. If you're in a similar situation where you and your siblings tend to agree and can work as a team, you can skip to the section below about what to discuss with your brother or sister before having a money talk with your parents.

But if you and your siblings are more likely to fight than agree, consider using an approach that Linda Fodrini-Johnson recommends. Fodrini-Johnson[2] is a licensed family therapist and founder of Eldercare Services in the San Francisco Bay Area. For more than three decades, she has worked with families who are caring for older adults and has had to help many family members put aside their differences and reach agreements on how to care for loved ones. Fortunately, her strategy for doing this is relatively easy to replicate.

Start by calling a meeting with your siblings, and let them know you want to talk to them about your parents' financial well-being. Ideally, you should gather in person rather than talk on the phone. Then ask your siblings to answer two questions:

About whom are you most concerned?

What would you like to get out of this meeting today?

Here's the really important part: Each person gets a chance to speak without questions or interruptions. The person who called the meeting should be the last person to answer the questions. And nobody can comment on what has been said until everyone has had a turn to talk.

Ideally, all of you will answer the first question by saying that you're most concerned about your parents. There's a good chance, though, you'll want to get different things out of the meeting. One sibling might say all of you should call a family meeting with your parents to discuss their finances while another might say you should butt out of your parents' money matters.

Instead of discussing the differences, focus first on what you agree on – that your top concern should be what's best for your parents. So rather than saying something like, "I can't believe you think Mom should stay in her house now that Dad's gone," you could say something like, "I'm glad we all agree that we should be concerned about mom. Let's talk more about what would be best for her." The goal is to find common ground.

WHAT TO DISCUSS WITH YOUR SIBLINGS

Before you have any conversations with your parents about their finances, you and your siblings should discuss and agree on several things. These are the key points you should bring up when you talk to them.

Who will initiate the conversation with your parents? You need to decide whether all of you want to approach your parents together or if it would be better to have just one of you initiate the conversation. If one of you is closer geographically or emotionally to your parents, you might agree that sibling is the right person for the job. If all of you are close to your parents and to each other, you might decide that a family meeting would be best.

However, you should give your parents a say in the matter. You could tell them that you and your siblings would like to have a family meeting to talk about their finances but that you'd like to know whether they'd feel more comfortable talking to one or all of you. Remember, the goal is to get them to talk, so their preferences should take precedence.

When will you have a conversation with your parents? If all of you plan to talk with your parents together, you might think that a holiday when the family is together would be ideal. However, this isn't a conversation you want to have during a holiday gathering. (I explain why in Chapter 7.) Try to find another time when all of you can sit down with Mom and Dad.

What approach will you use to get the conversation started? Again, if all siblings want to be present for the money talk with your parents, you need to agree on how to start the conversation. Ideally, you want to let your parents know that you appreciate everything they did for you and that you want to be able to help them if they ever need it. You can tell them that to do that, you'll need to gather some information from them. I provide a lot more detail in Chapter 7 on specific conversation starters you can use.

Who is willing to do what? Because your parents might need help from you someday, you and your siblings should discuss who is willing to do what. Then you'll avoid fights when a crisis arises because you'll already have agreed on what role each of you will play. Discuss who is willing to be involved with caregiving, who can provide financial support, and who would be willing to let a parent move in if necessary. Of course, your parents might have their own preferences. But you can let them know that you and your siblings have had conversations about what roles you think you're best able to fill.

Be aware that you might have a sibling who has a bad relationship with your parents and doesn't want to be involved. You have to be accepting of that, but you can ask if that sibling wants updates on your parents to stay in the loop. After all, that sibling might have a change of heart and want to get involved someday.

Exercise

Before talking to your siblings, make a list of the topics you'd like to discuss. You could use the points I've suggested that you address, or you could tailor my list to fit your family's situation. The point of putting something down in writing first is to give you an opportunity to think calmly and clearly about what you want to say. You could even send your siblings your list of the topics you want to address before you meet so they will be prepared to have a fruitful conversation.

NOTES

1. Kathy Kristof, http://www.kathykristof.com/about-me/ (Accessed Jan. 3, 2019).
2. Linda Fodrini-Johnson, https://eldercareanswers.com/about-us/meet-our-founder/ (Accessed Jan. 3, 2019).

CHAPTER 6

What Not to Say

I was watching the movie *Book Club* and got so mad at how the two daughters of Diane Keaton's character were treating her. Her character was recently widowed, and her daughters were convinced that she needed to move in with one of them. Never mind that she was capable of taking care of herself and would have to leave behind her tight-knit group of book club friends to move from California to Arizona, where her daughters lived. The daughters had decided what Mom should do and simply announced it to her. To top it off, they were condescending.

Yes, I know it's just a movie. But I realized that it was the perfect example of how not to talk to your parents. If you appear insensitive, controlling, or condescending when trying to start a conversation with your parents about their finances, they probably won't talk to you.

Remember how frustrated you felt when you were a teenager and thought you knew everything and your parents were constantly reminding you that you didn't? That's how they are going to feel if you start acting like the parent and treating them like naïve kids. No matter how much more you might know than Mom and Dad do about financial matters or how right you think you are about what is best for them, you have to remember that they are still the parents and you are still the child. You have to respect those roles if you want to have a productive conversation with them.

You also have to make sure you don't say or do the wrong things if you want to get your parents to open up to you about their finances. It might seem like I'm wagging my finger at you here, but the goal is to get your parents talking. So here's what you shouldn't do:

DON'T USE "YOU" LANGUAGE

If you start a conversation with your parents by saying, "You need to" or "You should," you put them on the defensive. "You've defined yourself as the superior one," said financial psychologist Dr. Mary Gresham.[1] And you're telling them what to do.

Rather than use "you," use "I" to get the conversation started, Gresham said. Try something like this:

> *I feel a need to know.*
> *I get concerned.*
> *I would like some information.*
> *I want to know the best way to care for you.*
> *I want to know what you really want.*

Therapists often use this approach[2] to avoid placing blame and to make it easier for clients to open up. By using "I," you are sharing how you feel rather than telling your parents what you expect them to do. As a result, you might have a better chance of getting them to empathize and understand why you want to gather information about their finances.

DON'T APPEAR TO HAVE SELFISH MOTIVES

Keep in mind that when you use "I" instead of "you" statements that you don't want appear to be acting in your own self-interest. If your parents think you're asking about their finances because you're being selfish, the conversation won't go well and they will probably shut down, said financial psychologist Dr. Brad Klontz.[3]

So starting a conversation with "Hey, can I see your will?" will probably make your parents think you're just interested in how much money they might be leaving you. You don't want to say anything that will be perceived as selfish. The better approach would be to express your concern that you want to make sure their wishes will be met, Klontz said. You could say something like, "I want to know how you want things handled if something happens to you."

Talking to your parents about whether they have an advance health care directive can be a good way to start a conversation because it puts the focus on what they want. This document spells out what medical treatment they would or would not want to prolong their lives and can also designate someone to make health care decisions if they are no longer able to themselves. If they don't have an advance directive, you can talk about why they need one, as well as other legal documents (which I explain in Chapter 10).

DON'T BE CONDESCENDING

You will sabotage any conversation with your parents about their finances the moment you become condescending. "You can't take the superior position," Gresham said. "Anybody is going to resist you."

Be aware that it's not just what you say that might come off as condescending, but also how you say it. If you speak slowly and use small words, your parents will feel like you're treating them like a preschooler, Gresham said. Talk to them as equals and give them the respect that you would want your kids to show to you someday if they try to have the same conversation with you.

DON'T FOCUS ONLY ON THE NEGATIVE

Admittedly, I am being negative here by telling you all of the things you shouldn't do. But my goal is to ensure that you don't wreck your chances of having a fruitful conversation with your parents by starting off on the wrong foot. One way that could happen is if you try to get your parents to open up about their finances by telling them all of the bad things that could happen if they don't.

It's okay if you want to use one worst-case scenario story – such as Doug's story in Chapter 4 – to highlight what could happen if you wait until it's too late to discuss things such as whom your parents want to be their power of attorney, whether they have a way to pay for long-term care, or even how to pay their bills for them if a health issue leaves them unable to do so. But don't dwell on the negative. Gresham recommends keeping the conversation focused on the positive – all of the good things that can come from having money talks sooner rather than later.

DON'T ISSUE ULTIMATUMS

If you get frustrated that your parents don't want to discuss their finances with you, don't try to force them to talk by giving them an ultimatum. In other words, don't say something like, "If you don't do this, I won't take care of you when you get older."

"That's not going to help build trust," Gresham said. Instead, ask them what little bit of information they might be willing to share, such as what bank they use. "You want to get one movement in the right direction," Gresham said. Then keep trying to get them to take small steps to reveal more details over time.

If they balk, then you might need to take a step back so you don't get in a power struggle. "If the first two passes haven't gotten anywhere, it's time to change your tactic," Gresham said. "Don't stay in the same conversation."

Keep in mind that you will need to be patient with your parents. It could take months or even years for them to feel comfortable enough to start sharing information with you that they consider to be private. If you push too hard, you could push them away. That's certainly not the goal.

The key is to give your parents time to come around and to keep the conversation focused on what's important to them – whether it's being able to live with dignity in their older years, being able to leave behind a legacy, or not being a burden on you. Hopefully they will realize that you have their best interests at heart and will open up to you rather than say, "I'm not having this conversation."

NOTES

1. Dr. Mary Gresham, http://doctorgresham.com/ (Accessed Jan. 3, 2019).
2. John A. Johnson (2012), "Are 'I' Statements Better Than 'You' Statements?" *Psychology Today*, https://www.psychologytoday.com/us/blog/cui-bono/201211/are-i-statements-better-you-statements (Accessed Jan. 2, 2019).
3. Dr. Brad Klontz, https://www.yourmentalwealth.com/about-us/dr-brad-klontz/ (Accessed Jan. 3, 2019).

CHAPTER 7

Conversation Starters

There is no one-size-fits-all approach to starting a conversation with your parents about their finances. That's why I'm giving you several tactics that both financial experts and ordinary folks like you have found to be successful in getting parents to open up about money matters.

If you're still on the fence about whether you want to go through with this, here's something very important to consider about why you need to have this conversation sooner rather than later. "You're either going to do it by plan or by crisis," financial psychologist Dr. Mary Gresham said. "It is going to happen." Ideally, you want it to happen when your parents are in good health, are mentally alert, and aren't an emotional mess (nor are you) because a crisis has struck.

The good news is that your parents probably won't resist your efforts to get them to share at least some of their financial information with you if you use one of the conversation starters I outline in this chapter. John Cooper,[1] a financial planner with Greenwood Capital, said he's learned by talking to many retirees that they recognize the importance of sharing financial information with their children. "There are really a lot of people out there who are interested in having these conversations with their children," he said. "They just need to be asked." So what are you waiting for?

WHEN TO HAVE THE CONVERSATION

Before you decide what you want to say to your parents, you need to figure out when to have a conversation with them. "Timing is really important," said eldercare expert Linda Fodrini-Johnson. Your efforts could backfire if you pick the wrong moment.

One of the worst times, for example, is during a holiday gathering. "Often kids will say, "We're all together. Let's talk to Mom now,'" Fodrini-Johnson said. "That's not okay. There's usually alcohol, little kids, and people who shouldn't hear the conversation are there." If the holidays are the only times when you and your parents gather, at least wait until the day after a family meal to try to talk to them about their finances. After all, how would you feel if someone asked you, "Could you please pass the turkey, then tell us who's going to get what when you die?"

You'll have much more success if you try to start a conversation with your parents at a time when everyone is relaxed and emotions aren't running high. If you have siblings and all of you want to be present, you need to decide jointly when you can gather to have a calm discussion that's free of distractions and time constraints. I know that's tough when we all have busy lives, but it's an important conversation that shouldn't be rushed.

It's also important to pick the right time of day to have this conversation if your parents have health issues or are showing signs of dementia, Fodrini-Johnson said. They're likely to be in a better mood and have more energy for this sort of discussion earlier in the day. But that could vary, so try to time your talk to coincide with the point in the day when they are functioning best.

Once you pinpoint a time to talk, you can use one of these strategies to get your parents to have a discussion with you. If they're willing to share details about their finances, see Chapter 9 for a list and explanation of the type of information you need to gather.

If the conversation you choose doesn't work, try another one. It might take time and several attempts to get your parents to open up to you. More importantly, don't push them to reveal more than they're comfortable discussing, said Josh Nelson,[2] founder and CEO of Keystone Financial Services. "It's probably a progression of conversations," he said. "This is probably not a one-time sit down, 'I'm going to spill my guts and tell you everything – now we're done.'"

As your parents do start to share information with you, take notes. You don't want to forget any details – which, trust me, you will if you don't keep a record of what your parents have told you.

10 TRIED-AND-TESTED CONVERSATION STARTERS

1. Use a Direct Approach

If you have a good relationship with your parents and they were relatively open about money matters while you were growing up, there's no need to beat around the bush. Simply let them know you would like to find out some information about their finances to give you peace of mind.

You don't necessarily have to ask them to tell you everything at once. Instead, you could start by asking about particular aspects of their finances. For example, when my mom started showing signs of memory loss, I suggested that we meet with an attorney to update her estate planning documents – her will, living will, and power of attorney. That then led to other conversations and a trip to her bank to put me on her account as her representative payee because I was going to have to handle financial transactions for her as her memory declined.

I really had no choice but to be direct with my mom because I had to act quickly before her Alzheimer's progressed too far. For the most part, she didn't push back because we had a good relationship, and she knew I had her best interests at heart. You'll likely have the same success I did if you and your parents get along, and you make it clear why you're trying to gather information from them about their finances.

2. Don't Make the Conversation About Money

I know it sounds crazy that I'm telling you not to talk about money in a book about how to have financial conversations with your parents, but hear me out. If your parents think money is a taboo topic, you'll be more likely to get them to open up about their finances if you start the conversation by talking about big-picture topics.

For example, you could casually ask, "Mom and Dad, have you given much thought to what your retirement will be like?" This will get them thinking – and, hopefully, talking – about what they want life to be like as they age. And their answers will likely give you clues to whether they're financially prepared for that lifestyle. If, say, they tell you that they'd love to be able to travel but that's not really in the cards, then it might be a clue that they don't have much money set aside for retirement. You could respond by saying something like, "That's too bad. Why don't you think you'll be able to travel?" or "Are you sure? There are plenty of cheap ways to travel." Then you could offer to help them brainstorm ways to find room in their budget to afford to travel or do the things they want in retirement, which might give you more insight into their finances.

Another way to approach the conversation without initially making it about money is to ask your parents about their wishes. The point is to show them you're concerned about being able to uphold those wishes, whether it's the type of care they would want later in life, end-of-life care, or their final wishes. For example, you could say, "Mom and Dad, you took such good care of me when I was younger. I want to be able to provide that same sort of care if you ever need it." This could open the door to conversations about whether they have a will, a living will, financial and health care power of attorney documents, or a plan for long-term care.

3. Send an Invitation

It might seem old-fashioned to send your parents an invitation to talk, but it can be a polite gesture that an older generation will appreciate. And it's more likely to result in a productive conversation. "It's really helpful to let your parents know you want to have this conversation in writing rather than catch them in the moment when they have to give you an immediate response," said financial psychologist Dr. Mary Gresham.

"The immediate response is going to be more emotional. If you write to them and say, 'I want to invite you to have this talk with me,' that gives them time to work through their emotions."

Explain in your letter what you want to discuss. And let your parents know that you're inviting them to have this conversation out of love – your love and desire to be able to help them as they age and their love and willingness to share information with you so you *can* help them if they need it.

The benefit of an invitation is that it lets your parents maintain a sense of control. "An invitation is different from a demand or a request," Gresham said. "People process the word 'invitation' differently." You are asking kindly to have a conversation but giving them the option to decide whether to accept your invitation. And you can let them decide when and where to meet to have the conversation by asking parents to share a vision of what will make it work for them, Gresham said. "If they say, 'Never,' you can always say, 'That doesn't work for me,'" she said.

4. Ask for Advice

As I wrote in Chapter 3, some parents might be reluctant to have money talks with their children because they feel like it's a reversal of roles. If you suspect that will be the case with your parent, start the conversation by asking for help with your own financial matters. For example, you could tell your parent that you want advice on how to save for retirement, whether you need a will, or how much life insurance you should get now that you have a family of your own.

"Tell them what you're thinking about doing so you give them the power to tell you what they think you should do," said Daniel Lash,[3] a certified financial planner with VLP Financial Advisors. "It's like they're giving you advice because that's what parents are good at – giving advice."

The goal in asking your parents to give you advice is to get them to open up about the financial and estate planning they have done. For example, they might tell you that they didn't have to worry about saving for retirement because they will get a pension. You could keep the conversation going by saying, "Wow, you're lucky. Have you had to do anything else to make sure you'll have a comfortable retirement, like getting long-term care insurance or planning to downsize to a smaller home?"

If you ask whether you should have a will and they tell you they never bothered to get one, you could suggest that all of you meet with an attorney together to draft wills.

5. Use a Story

Stories are a great way to get a conversation going with your parents about their finances. You could tell them about a friend whose father died without a will and the family ended up in court fighting over who got what because the father had been married more than once and had stepchildren who wanted a piece of the pie. Then you could ask whether they've done any estate planning to prevent this sort of situation.

You could tell them about a colleague whose mother had a stroke that left her hospitalized, and the friend couldn't access any of the mom's financial accounts to pay bills because they had never planned for this sort of situation. Then you could discuss the importance of naming a power of attorney to make financial decisions for them if they can't (which I'll discuss in more detail in Chapter 10) and creating a list of financial accounts and passwords.

Or you could tell them about a neighbor whose parent was a victim of identity theft and that you want to help protect them. You could then show them how to log onto AnnualCreditReport.com to get a free copy of their credit report, which you could review with them for signs of fraud, such as accounts they didn't open (and get good insight into the types of accounts they have).

If you don't have a story of your own to share, you can borrow one. For example, you could use Doug Nordman's from Chapter 4. Or you could make up one that's tailored to the type of financial information you want to get from your parents. I know it feels a little sleazy to lie, but this is a white lie that can help you get important information about your parents' finances. Remember, though, that you don't want to drone on about all of the bad things that have happened to families who didn't discuss financial matters. Share one story, then focus on how having conversations sooner rather than later can help ensure that it will be easier for everyone – you, your siblings, Mom or Dad – down the road.

6. Talk About Your Own Financial Planning Experience

Plenty of financial advisers say that talking about your own financial planning experience can be a good way to get your parents to open up about theirs. Nelson said he often recommends to clients that they get their own estate planning done, then use that as a conversation starter with their parents. For example, you could tell your parents that you recently had a will drafted and want them to know where they can find it if something happens to you.

Hopefully, your parents will then let you know if they have a will or other estate planning documents and where they are. If not, Nelson recommended that you take the opportunity to ask. Or you could tell them that you recently met with a financial planner or took some other step to make a financial plan. You could share how helpful the experience was for you and ask whether they've done anything similar.

7. Use a Life Event

A life event – either one in your family or in another family you know well – can help start a conversation with your parents about what they've done to prepare for events that will happen in their lives, said Marguerita Cheng,[4] a financial planner and CEO of Blue Ocean Global Wealth. For example, you could say something like, "I've seen how hard Grandma's death has been for you, and it got me thinking. What sort of planning have you done?"

You don't have to wait for a death in the family, though. A marriage, divorce, graduation, or birth of a baby could be used to start the conversation. The point is to use a life event to talk about being proactive so your parents can have more control over what happens to their finances and any assets they might leave behind when they die. You can tell your parents that you know that it might be a difficult conversation to have, Cheng said. But she said you should then say, "If something happens, we don't want to have to make these decisions for you."

You could suggest that they check their financial accounts and life insurance policies to make sure their beneficiaries are updated. You could ask them to consider meeting with an attorney to draft or update their estate planning documents. Or you could gently nudge them to discuss what sort of long-term care they would want if they ever needed it. Even if you get them to take baby steps, that's a good start, Cheng said.

8. Use Current Events

Chances are, you and your parents discuss current events from time to time. When financial topics are in the news –changes to the tax law, big swings in the stock market, health care reform, the list goes on – use that as a launching point for a conversation about your parents' finances.

For example, Jason – a 40-something who lives in California – used the poor state of the economy during the Great Recession to start a conversation with his mom about how it was affecting her finances. He was in his 30s at the time, and she was in her 60s, going into semi-retirement. "I mainly asked her if she had been speaking with anyone about her retirement funds and if she had moved any of her holdings into a safe harbor type of situation to prevent any negative fallout from the market crash in 2008–2009." He then asked her how she felt about her savings and whether she was prepared for retirement. Jason learned that she had been talking to her financial advisor about these topics and was taking steps to protect her savings. Since that initial conversation, he has had more with her and continues to check in to see how she's doing financially.

9. Ask About "What If" Scenarios

One of the key reasons to talk to your parents about their finances is to be prepared for emergencies. So asking them about "what if" scenarios might lead to more in-depth planning and preparation. For example, you could ask what would happen if both of them ended up in the hospital after a car accident. Let them know that someone would have to be designated as a health care power of attorney to speak with their doctors and make medical decisions for them if they couldn't on their own. And someone would have to be designated as power of attorney to handle financial transactions for them, such as paying bills. Most likely, it will be a relief to them that you're asking and want to plan for worst-case scenarios, said Jan Valecka,[5] a financial planner and owner of Valecka Wealth Management.

You also could ask your parents to share details about their final wishes. "It can be as simple as, 'Do you want a burial or a cremation?'" Valecka said. If they are reluctant to answer, let them know that you need to know so you don't have to make this sort of decision for them. If they don't want to hand over detailed information to you about their finances to prepare for worst-case scenarios, ask them to make a list of the accounts, insurance policies, and legal documents they have and to tell you where you could find that list if something happens.

10. Offer to Lighten Their Load

You can gain insight into your parents' finances by offering to take over a financial task for them so they have more time to do what they enjoy. This is a good strategy to use if you haven't had any money talks with your parents and they already are showing signs that they're having trouble managing their finances on their own.

You could start small by suggesting that you help them set up automatic bill payments. They might not even use their bank's website, so this would give you a chance to create an online account for them, and to keep tabs on their account going forward. Or you could offer to tackle one of the most universally dreaded financial tasks for them – tax preparation. You don't necessarily have to prepare their tax return for them. Instead, you could help them gather their documents and take them to an accountant to prepare their return. In the process, though, you'll get details of their finances that you'll need if you ever have to manage all money matters for them.

ABOVE ALL, REMAIN CALM AND RESPECTFUL

Regardless of the conversation starter you choose to use, remember to be respectful when talking to your parents. As I wrote in Chapter 6, you won't get very far if you're condescending. So come at this conversation from a place of compassion and reverence for your parents, even if that's not truly how you feel. You're more likely to have success if you're talking *with* them rather than at them. After all, the goal is to have a conversation, not a monologue.

Also keep your emotions in check as you have this conversation with your parents. The reason you're trying to have this talk with Mom or Dad before a crisis strikes is to do it when everyone is calm and level-headed. So if they balk at your efforts to get them to open up, don't let your frustration get the best of you.

Exercise

Now it's time to decide which conversation starter will work best with your parents. You might even want to pick a couple that you want to try. Then craft a dialogue.

You could simply list key talking points or questions to ask. Or you could write what you want to say word for word. It might seem like overkill, but putting your thoughts into writing will help you get clear on what you want to say. It could also help you anticipate your parents' reactions to your line of questioning so you'll be prepared with responses to get the most out of the conversation or to encourage them to open up if they're reluctant to talk.

NOTES

1. John Cooper, http://wealth.greenwoodcapital.com/our-team/john-w-cooper-cfp (Accessed Jan. 3, 2019).

2. Josh Nelson, https://www.keystonefinancial.com/team-members/josh-nelson/ (Accessed Jan. 3, 2019).
3. Daniel Lash, http://www.vlpfa.com/team/daniel-p-lash-cfp-aif (Accessed Jan. 3, 2019).
4. Marguerita Cheng, https://www.blueoceanglobalwealth.com/our-team.html (Accessed Jan. 3, 2019).
5. Jan Valecka, https://janvalecka.advisorwebsite.com/ (Accessed Jan. 3, 2019).

A Step-by-Step Approach to a Successful Conversation

When Ryan Inman's stepdad had a stroke, it caught his mom off guard. Although Jimmy, his stepdad, was 70, he was in great shape because he worked out three hours every day by lifting weights and running. And Michelle, Ryan's mom, thought she had a handle on their finances.

But when the stroke landed Jimmy in the hospital and the doctors discovered he had bone cancer, Ryan said it became obvious that his mom hadn't taken steps to organize the couple's finances to deal with an emergency like this. As a certified financial planner and founder of Physician Wealth Services,[1] Ryan wanted to talk to his mom about her lack of planning but knew it wasn't the right time because she was struggling emotionally with her husband's diagnosis.

Fortunately, Jimmy beat the cancer. But Ryan said that his mom and stepdad never took the time to get financially organized to prepare for another emergency. That worried him because he had seen how hard it had been for them before when they weren't prepared and could see that Jimmy's health was deteriorating, which meant they could end up in the same situation once again.

Ryan knew it was time to have that talk with his mom about her finances that he had wanted to have when his stepdad had a stroke. This time, there was no excuse not to have it. "You can always say there's never a right time, but there's never a wrong time, other than during a crisis," he said.

Indeed, Ryan did have a conversation with his mom – several, actually – and it went incredibly well. He admits that being a financial planner helped him know what to ask his mom about her finances and, more importantly, how to ask. Because his approach was carefully planned, it's worth replicating when talking with your parents about their finances.

Of course, everyone's situation is different. But following Ryan's step-by-step approach that helped him have successful conversations with his mom about her finances might work for you.

STEP 1: CHOOSE THE RIGHT TIME AND PLACE TO BROACH THE TOPIC

Ideally, you want to talk with your parents about their finances before a crisis strikes. As Ryan witnessed, emotions are running high when there's an emergency, so it can be difficult – or even impossible – to gather the information you need at that time.

Instead, choose a time to bring up the topic of money when your parents are relaxed and in a good mood. Ryan decided to start asking his mom about how prepared she was for another emergency while he was visiting her with his two young children. "She's got the grandkids around, so she was in a good mood," he said. "I made it so she was very comfortable in a setting that was her own and brought over her two favorite people in the world."

STEP 2: EXPLAIN WHY YOU WANT TO HAVE THE CONVERSATION

While relaxing with his mom and watching his kids play, Ryan casually mentioned to her that he had recently talked to her husband, Jimmy, and that he didn't sound too good. He then asked whether they had everything in order if something were to happen to Jimmy.

"I was like, 'You know, Mom, do you have stuff together? I want to make sure your will is together because Jimmy is starting to fail. It could be a year, it could be 10 years." He told her they needed to get all of their estate planning documents updated and to go over all of the accounts she and her husband had while he still was coherent. "I told her, 'This isn't for me to figure out what I'm going to get or not get. You just need to be prepared. We need to make sure everything is taken care of,'" Ryan said.

The key is to let your parents know you want to talk about their finances so you can help them plan and be prepared. Don't focus on what you hope to get out of the conversation, Ryan said. Instead, tell them you want to help them make sure everything is in order now to make it easier for them if something happens.

STEP 3: FIND A QUESTION TO PROMPT THEM TO TALK

On the one hand, Ryan said it was easy to bring up the topic of finances with his mom because money has never been a taboo topic in his family. However, he doesn't think she would have been willing to have more conversations and share details of her finances if he hadn't asked her the right question.

Ryan knew that his mom and stepdad had a prenuptial agreement and separate financial accounts. So when he started talking to her about whether they had their finances in order, Ryan asked his mom if she knew what financial accounts his step-dad had and where they were. "I think when I asked her does he still have separate property, she didn't know," Ryan said. "That was a prompting question to get her intrigued into thinking, 'Uh oh, maybe I don't know everything. Let's look at it.'"

Ryan recommends finding a prompting question you could ask your parents to get them thinking about why it's important that they discuss their finances with you. Using a story, a life event, or any of the other conversation starters in Chapter 7 also can help. "That's your door in to talking about it," he said. Then you could offer to help them get organized or make a plan *in case* something happens (which it will, but you don't need to scare your parents by pointing out that they will die, could have serious health issues, or end up needing long-term care).

STEP 4: SCHEDULE A TIME TO TALK IN DEPTH

Once his mom agreed that they needed to look into her and her husband's financial situation more, Ryan didn't start prodding her for information. "I said, 'Mom, if you want to talk about this, let's do it when the kids aren't around. Let's set up a time,'" he said. Then Ryan got out his calendar and scheduled a time to meet with his mom to discuss her finances. So she wouldn't feel overwhelmed, though, he told her they would only talk about 20 to 30 minutes.

STEP 5: START WITH THE EASY STUFF

Ryan went to his mother's house for their first scheduled money conversation and started with questions about banking that he knew she could answer. He asked at which bank she had accounts, what sort of accounts she had, and how many accounts she had. "Start with the easy stuff first," Ryan said. "That's an easy win."

He never once asked about how much money she had in her accounts. In fact, he told his mom he didn't care about the dollar amount – only about the type and number of accounts she had. However, he did create an account on Dropbox.com, which lets you share files easily with other people. He asked his mom to download her most recent bank statement that listed the accounts she had, along with the account numbers, and save them in a Dropbox file so that he could access it if it ever was necessary. "That way I know where it's at if something happens to her so I can help," he said.

STEP 6: DO IT OVER MULTIPLE CONVERSATIONS

Ryan didn't ask his mom to share all of the details of her finances in a single meeting. In fact, he met with his mom several times over the course of three months, which is what he recommends that others do, too. "Take it in small doses," he said. "After a certain amount of time, you get tired. People who really don't like talking about it will get tired really quick."

Each time Ryan and his mom met, he focused on only one aspect of her finances. After they talked about banking during their first meeting, he then asked her about her debt. Ryan found out that his mother didn't have any. But if she did, he would have asked her to list all of her lines of credit and what she owed.

Next, he asked about her investments, which was a more challenging conversation because his mother has several investment accounts and investment properties. Plus, she didn't know what accounts her husband had, so Ryan had to ask his stepdad to share that information with them.

Ryan then made a list of all of his mom's and her husband's investment accounts and got account statements to save in the Dropbox file. He also had his mom make a list of all of her rental properties with details such as addresses, property managers, and names of tenants for each.

In other meetings, he focused on cash flow – what sources of income his mom and stepdad have. "I told her, 'You don't have to tell me the numbers. I just need to know that you know where it's coming from,'" Ryan said. However, he did ask her to make a detailed list of income sources in a Word document and save it in the Dropbox. He also gathered information about all of the insurance policies – auto, homeowners, life, and so on – that his mom and stepdad have and asked them to put digital copies of their policies in the Dropbox.

STEP 7: LISTEN WITHOUT BIAS AND WRITE DOWN EVERYTHING

As you talk with your parents about their finances, Ryan cautions that it's important not to pass any judgment on them. As you know, talking about money can be difficult for many people. It might be especially hard for your parents if they are embarrassed about their financial situation. "You just have to ask the questions and listen," Ryan said.

As you listen, though, write down any important financial information your parents share with you, such as the types of accounts they have. Ryan recommends taking notes with a pen and paper rather than a computer because typing information into a computer will make the conversation feel more formal. "You want to make them as comfortable as you possibly can while talking through something uncomfortable," he said. You can always go back and transcribe your notes on a computer in a Word or Excel file. If your parents aren't comfortable sharing specific details about their accounts, debts, insurance policies, or estate planning documents, you could ask them to write down that information themselves and store it someplace where you could access it if there is an emergency and you need it to help them. For more details on the type of information you need to collect, see Chapter 9. You also can find a downloadable fill-in-the-blank "In Case of Emergency" organizer at Cameron Huddleston.com that you can use or give to your parents to fill out and store in a safe place.

STEP 8: FIND A WAY TO MAKE THE HARDER CONVERSATIONS EASIER

Ryan saved the toughest conversation with his mom for last – the conversation about end-of-life planning. "It's a harder conversation because you don't want to seem like the kid who wants to know what their inheritance is," Ryan said. And, of course, that wasn't his goal. He simply wanted to find out whether his mom had recorded her final wishes. He also wanted to make sure that she and her husband had health care directives that spelled out what sort of end-of-life care they wanted and that named financial and health care power of attorneys to make decisions for them if they couldn't.

To help keep the conversation more relaxed, he took his mom to lunch and didn't take notes. "I said, 'Look, this isn't for me, it's for you. When Jimmy dies, you'll not only be grieving, you're going to have a lot of work. Let's get this work done now when it's easy and you're not in a different state of mind,'" Ryan said. He also pointed out that this was something his mom and her husband needed to do before Jimmy's mental and physical health declined more. For legal documents to be valid, a person has to be mentally competent to sign them.

As they talked, Ryan found out that his mom and stepdad had wills and financial power of attorneys that hadn't been updated in a while. Plus, neither had an advance health care directive. Ryan told his mom that it was imperative that they both have this essential document drafted to detail the type of treatments (such as life support) they would or would not want to receive if a medical emergency left them unable to communicate their wishes. Without those documents, their loved ones wouldn't know what they wanted, he said. Ryan told his mom that she didn't have to tell him right then what she wanted but that she needed to think about it and meet with an estate planning attorney.

"I put the harder questions on the estate planning attorney," Ryan said. "I wanted a third party to get the answers to those questions."

He also told her what sort of other information the estate planning attorney would want so she could be prepared to provide it when she met with one. Fortunately, she had already gathered most of that information during her money conversations with Ryan and stored it in Dropbox files.

Within two months after their lunch meeting, Ryan's mom had met with an attorney and had signed all of the estate planning documents she needed. She emailed Ryan her attorney's contact information, whom he can contact if there is an emergency and he needs access to the documents. "I now know she got everything done according to her wishes," Ryan said.

(Note: Most attorneys do not keep original versions of estate planning documents that they draft on file. So don't expect that your parents' attorney will have their documents. Even if they do have them on file, they likely won't be able to give them to you unless you've been named your parent's power of attorney.)

NOTE

1. Ryan Inman, https://physicianwealthservices.com/ (Accessed Jan. 3, 2019).

CHAPTER 9

What You Need to Know

It's time to dig deep into your parents' financial situation. Of course, the amount of information you can gather will depend on what they're willing to share. That's why I've developed lists of what you need to find out to correspond with the varying levels of comfort your parents might exhibit in opening up to you. Ideally, you want to collect as much detail about your parents' finances as possible so you can be prepared to help if they're ever unable to manage their finances on their own. But you might need to tread carefully and gather information over time as your parents get more comfortable with the idea of sharing the facets of their finances with you.

In addition to the detailed lists in this chapter, a downloadable "In Case of Emergency" organizer is available at Cameron Huddleston.com for readers to print and give to parents to complete. This chapter also should help anyone who feels like a novice when it comes money matters get a better understanding of personal finance basics.

FOR RELUCTANT PARENTS: START WITH THE BASICS

Parents who aren't comfortable talking about money might not be willing to share a lot of details about their finances. And that's okay. You don't want to push too hard and sabotage your chances of getting them to give you any information. But there are a few key things you should try to find out to avoid a financial mess if an emergency strikes or when they die. Make it clear that you're asking that they share this information so all of you can be prepared for worst-case scenarios. Here are the questions you should ask.

Do you have a will or living trust? Let your parents know that you're not asking this question to find out whether you're getting an inheritance. You simply want to make sure that they have a written plan for what happens to their assets when they die. Without a will or living trust, the laws in their state and a judge will determine what happens to their property and assets. Going through the legal process to sort this out can make a tough time even harder for loved ones they leave behind. So if your parents want a say in who gets what – even if they don't have much – they need one of these legal documents. For a lot more detail on wills and trusts, see Chapter 10. If your parents already have a will or living trust, ask them where it is stored so you can access it when the time comes. Also ask who they have named as the executor – the person who is entrusted with settling their estate when they die. If that person is you, you and your parents will need to talk more about what your duties will be as an executor.

Do you have a power of attorney? I can't emphasize enough how important it is for your parents to designate a power of attorney while they are healthy and of sound mind. This legal document – which they can have drafted by an attorney – allows them to designate someone to make financial decisions for them if they cannot. For a power of attorney document to be valid, the person signing it must be mentally competent. If something were to happen to your parents (such as a stroke, coma, or dementia) and they hadn't named a power of attorney, someone would have to go through expensive legal proceedings to be appointed by a judge to make financial decisions for them. Chapter 10 has more details about the various types of power of attorney. If your parents already have designated someone to be their power of attorney, it would be helpful to know whether you're that person and where their POA documents are.

Do you have an advance health care directive? If the answer is no, explain to your parents that this document – also called a living will – allows them to spell out what sort of medical care and end-of-life support they want if they're unable to make decisions for themselves. An advance health care directive also lets them name someone – a health care surrogate or proxy – to make medical decisions for them if they can't. If they don't have advance health care directives, you and your siblings will likely have to make decisions about life support for your parents without knowing what they want. Or a court might even appoint someone to make health care decisions for your parents. The National Hospice and Palliative Care Organization provides free downloadable state-specific advance directives at www.caringinfo.org. However, it's a good idea to meet with an attorney to draft a more detailed advance directive. Again, I provide more detail about advance directives in Chapter 10.

How do you pay your bills? Like the other three questions, this one is important to ask because it will help avoid a financial mess if something happens to your parents. And that's how you should frame it when you're asking this. You want to find out whether they use automatic bill pay or write checks every month. If it's the latter, take the opportunity to recommend that your parents automate as many bills as possible to ensure that they always get paid on time. Point out that it's one less thing they'll have to worry about every month. You could even offer to help them set up automatic bill pay, which will give you insight into their monthly expenses. If they resist, let them know that you won't be able to pay bills for them if something happens unless they've named you as power of attorney and have told you where to find their POA documents, which you'll need to provide to the bank. Their bank might also require that you be listed as a representative payee on their account to sign checks for them. If your parents are showing signs of dementia, you'll need to visit their bank with them as soon as possible to be listed on their account as a representative payee. If they're in good health and still relatively young, you don't need to insist that your parents take this step at this time.

Do what you can to get answers to these four questions. At least if you know that your parents have estate planning documents, you won't have to worry about whether they've spelled out their final wishes and have named people to make financial and health care decisions for them. And if you know that their bills are paid automatically, that's one less thing to worry about if something happens to them. If your parents don't have estate planning documents – especially power of attorney – warn them that family members might have to go through a lengthy and expensive legal process to get the authority to access their accounts and pay their bills if a health condition leaves them unable to handle their finances on their own.

WHEN THEY'RE READY TO SHARE MORE

Knowing basic information such as whether your parents have essential legal documents will help make things a little easier if an emergency were to strike. But to really be able to step in and help if a health issue lands them in the hospital or if they develop dementia, you'll need more details about their finances. This information is also important to find out if you suspect that they are struggling financially and might need support from you as they age.

- **Sources of income**: If your parents are still working, obviously they have income from their jobs or businesses they own. However, they might also have income from investments such as dividend-paying stocks or rental property. Other sources of income could include disability benefits if they were injured and no longer able to work. If they are retired, common sources of income include Social Security benefits, pension benefits from a former employer, military retirement pay, veteran pension, retirement savings accounts such as a 401(k) or IRA, annuities, and nonretirement accounts such as certificates of deposit and brokerage accounts. Ask your parents to tell you or make a list of all of their sources of income, pointing out that you'll need to know this information if they ever need your help with their finances. If your parents are planning on retiring soon but don't know what their monthly Social Security benefit amount will be, they can find out by creating an online "my Social Security" account at www.ssa.gov/signin. If they don't have an online account, the Social Security Administration does mail statements[1] to workers age 60 and older three months before their birthday or upon request. They can visit a local office or call 800-772-1213[2] for help.

- **Bank accounts**: Find out where your parents bank and the types of accounts they have, such as checking and savings accounts. (And, no, you don't need to ask how much they have in their accounts). Also find out if your parents have joint or separate bank accounts. If something were to happen to one of your parents, you want to ensure that the other parent has access to cash to pay bills. If the accounts aren't joint, the healthy or surviving parent could have trouble getting the money he or she needs.
- **Household debt**: You don't necessarily need to find out how much your parents owe, but it would helpful to know what types of debt they have. Do they have a mortgage, car loans, personal loans, or business loans? What credit cards do they have, and are they carrying balances on those cards? Do they have medical debt? Are they still paying your student loans or their own? If your parents are unsure about the types and amounts of debt they have, they can get a complete list of their credit accounts on their credit report from any of the three credit bureaus – Experian, Equifax, and TransUnion. They can get a free copy of their credit report from the credit bureaus once a year at www.annualcreditreport.com.
- **Monthly bills**: Ideally, you should get a list of all of the monthly bills they pay, not just information about how they pay their bills. Having this list will help you ensure that all of their bills get paid if they are unable to pay them for whatever reason. In addition to bills for essentials such as water and electricity, you also need to know whether they have monthly subscription services such as cable or satellite TV, cell phone, video streaming, or credit monitoring.
- **Insurance policies**: Find out what types of insurance policies they have (homeowners, auto, umbrella liability, life,

health, disability, and long-term care), which companies
issued the policies, the names of their insurance agents,
and how the premiums are paid. Ask them where they
store their policies. Also make sure they've listed beneficiaries for any life insurance policies they have.

- **Investment accounts:** Ask your parents whether they
have brokerage accounts for investments such as stocks,
bonds, and mutual funds. These would be accounts
other than retirement accounts and would be with an
investment firm or bank. Get the names of the financial
institutions where they have investment accounts.

- **Real estate:** Get a description of the real estate they own,
including addresses, property managers, and whether
they have outstanding property loans.

- **Financial professionals:** Get names and contact information for any professionals they work with, such as attorneys, accountants, or financial planners.

- **Final wishes:** Tell your parents that you want to know
whether they have any preferences for their funeral and
burial so that you can uphold their final wishes. In fact,
ask them to put their final wishes in writing so there
won't be any question about what they want. Also be sure
to ask whether they have prepaid for their funerals. If
so, find out which funeral home or insurance company
issued the prepaid funeral policy. If they haven't, don't
encourage them to prepay for their funerals because the
Funeral Consumers Alliance[3] cautions against it. Often,
the premiums cost more than the policy will pay at the
time of death. And if your parents die within a few years
after getting a policy, the insurance company might not
pay the full benefit.

GET ALL THE ESSENTIAL INFORMATION YOU NEED

If your parents are an open book, ask them to share the
following specific details about their finances. If it makes them
more comfortable, tell them to write down this information
or use the downloadable "In Case of Emergency" organizer at

CameronHuddleston.com, store it in a safe place, and let you know how to access it if something happens to them. However, I do know parents who willingly hand over this information to their children. I have a friend whose parents give her an updated list of their financial information every six months.

If your parents do give you a detailed list of financial accounts and information, be sure to **store it in a safe place** that can only be accessed by you and others who are authorized to see it. This is very sensitive information that could be used to steal your parents' identity if it fell into the wrong hands.

Detailed financial information to gather:

- Social Security numbers
- Medicare or Medicaid numbers (The U.S. Centers for Medicare and Medicaid Services sent new Medicare cards to Medicare recipients in late 2018[4] with new Medicare numbers rather than Social Security numbers on the cards. Old cards should be destroyed. More information about the new cards is available at www.medicare.gov.)
- Driver's license numbers
- Military ID
- Account numbers, passwords, and usernames for all financial accounts
- Usernames and passwords for subscription services such as Netflix and Amazon Prime (you'll need to be able to cancel these when your parents die)
- Usernames and passwords for social media accounts
- Locations of keys to house and any other properties
- Location of checks, debit cards, and credit cards
- Location of keys for bank lockboxes
- Location of home safes and the keys or combinations for those safes
- Location of property deeds and appraisals
- Location of automobile titles
- Location of stock or bond certificates
- Location of past tax returns and current year tax documents, receipts, and the like
- Location of valuables such as jewelry and silver

- Location of business contracts
- Current employer and employment history

Other essential information to gather:

- Your parents' birthdates (if you never can seem to remember them)
- Names and contact information of their doctors, dentists, and therapists
- Allergies
- List of medications, dosages, prescribing doctor, and pharmacy
- Medical conditions (diabetes, high blood pressure, and so on)
- Medical history (get dates of any surgeries or procedures, if possible)
- Location of Do Not Resuscitate Order (might be included in advance health care directive)
- Emergency contacts
- Location of birth certificates
- Location of marriage license or divorce decree
- Location of military service records
- Place of worship
- Instructions for caring for pets
- List of your parents' friends they want notified of their death
- List of accomplishments, involvements to be included in their obituaries

HOW HAVING THIS INFORMATION WILL HELP

As I mentioned earlier in this book, one of my biggest regrets is not having conversations sooner with my mom about her finances. Fortunately, she had named me and my sister as power of attorney and health care proxy while she was still competent. However, once her memory started slipping, I had to step in and start helping her with money matters. It was tough getting all of the information I needed about her accounts from her because of her dementia. So I had to play detective by going through her wallet, her mail, her tax files, and her bank account statements. I felt sleazy, but I didn't have a choice. I needed all of those details – including her Social Security number – to reach out to her financial institutions to be listed as the power of attorney on her accounts, to make financial and health care decisions for her, to file tax returns for her, and to interact with the Social Security Administration on her behalf.

If your parents ever have a health crisis that forces you to step in and help, you will need most of the information in this chapter that I have suggested you gather. Without it, you'll find it incredibly difficult to help them. Even if they remain healthy, you'll need this information when they die to close accounts, to collect life insurance benefits, and to ensure that their wishes are followed.

Gathering this information also will give you insight into whether your parents will have enough money to get by in retirement. For example, if you learn that they've been working with a financial planner or have a detailed plan for retirement, you can breathe a sigh of relief that they'll likely be okay. But if you find out that their only source of income in retirement will be Social Security, be aware that they might have a hard time getting by – especially if they have debt.

The average monthly Social Security retirement benefit is only $1,413.[5] If both of your parents are receiving that much each month, it could be enough to live comfortably if they no longer have a mortgage and other consumer debt – and don't end up needing long-term care. But the average Social Security check might not be enough to sustain your parents if they have mortgage or other debt, have serious health issues, or are in a city with a high cost of living. You might want to suggest that they work longer and wait to start collecting Social Security benefits. For every year they wait to collect benefits[6] past their full retirement age until age 70, they can increase the amount they get. Currently the maximum payout beneficiaries can get if they wait until age 70 is about $3,700. Of course, health issues might prevent your parents from working longer, and they might not be able to wait to claim Social Security benefits. The point is that they should research their options before applying for benefits to get the most out of Social Security. The Social Security Administration has a variety of calculators to help your parents plan at https://www.ssa.gov/planners/calculators/.

You also might need to discuss with your parents the financial benefits of downsizing to a smaller home in retirement. (See Chapter 13 for tips on talking to your parents about when it's time to move.) If your parents truly are struggling, you might have to examine your own finances – and your willingness to get involved – to see if you'll be able to afford to help them out if necessary.

The sooner you have conversations with your parents, the more time you'll have to plan and to help them take necessary steps to improve their financial situation. However, if that ship has sailed and they're already retired with a limited income, there are resources that can help:

- **American Association of Daily Money Managers**: Some members of this organization volunteer their services to help low-income people with money management. The association's website has a list of state agencies that provide daily money management services at https://secure.aadmm.com/state-agencies/.
- **National Council on Aging**: This organization has a wealth of information on its website, www.ncoa.org, to help older adults stay economically secure as they age. Its free BenefitsCheckUp service (www.benefitscheckup.org) helps seniors find out what benefit programs they might be eligible for to save money on health care, medication, food, housing, utilities, and more.
- **National Foundation for Credit Counseling**: This nonprofit financial counseling organization has a network of member agencies serving all 50 states. If your parents are struggling with debt, they can get free or low-cost credit and debt counseling from NFCC member agencies by calling 800-388-2227 or using the NFCC counselor locator online at www.nfcc.org/locator/.
- **Senior Service America**: This nonprofit organization operates the Senior Community Service Employment

Program and other programs for older workers. If your parents need help finding work to make ends meet, they might get it through Senior Service America programs (www.seniorserviceamerica.org/).

NOTES

1. Social Security Administration (2018), "How Can I Get a Social Security Statement That Shows a Record of My Earnings and Estimate of My Future Benefits?" https://faq.ssa.gov/en-US/Topic/article/KA-01741 (Accessed Jan. 3, 2019).
2. Social Security Administration, "Request for a Social Security Statement," https://www.ssa.gov/hlp/global/hlp-statement-7004.htm (Accessed Jan. 3, 2019).
3. Funeral Consumers Alliance, "Should You Prepay for Your Funeral? Safer Ways to Plan Ahead," https://funerals.org/?consumers=should-you-prepay-for-your-funeral (Accessed Jan. 3, 2019).
4. Medicare.gov, https://www.medicare.gov/newcard/ (Accessed Jan. 3, 2019).
5. Social Security Administration (2018), "Fact Sheet," https://www.ssa.gov/news/press/factsheets/basicfact-alt.pdf (Accessed Jan. 3, 2019).
6. Social Security Administration, "Delayed Retirement Credits," https://www.ssa.gov/planners/retire/delayret.html (Accessed Jan. 3, 2019).

10

Talking to Your Parents About Estate Planning Documents

To be clear, this chapter isn't designed to help you have a conversation with your parents about whether you're getting an inheritance. In fact, plenty of financial planners have told me that some parents tend to be reluctant to have financial conversations with their children because they don't want to discuss the topic of inheritance. Parents don't want their kids to think they can coast through life because they know they'll get a windfall someday. Or they don't want their children to be upset if they're planning on giving more to one kid than the others.

More importantly, you shouldn't even be counting on getting an inheritance. Assume you're getting nothing and take steps to secure your own finances. Then if you do get something, think of it as icing on the cake.

So why then should you talk to your parents about whether they have estate planning documents? For starters, you want to make sure they have legal documents that spell out *their* wishes. It's about what they want, not what you hope to get. And, hopefully, by spelling out what they want, it will make things easier for loved ones they leave behind.

Plus, estate planning goes well beyond wills. It includes essential legal documents your parents need to ensure someone can make financial and health care decisions for them if they are unable to do so themselves. In fact, I'd say that these documents – power of attorney and advance health care directive – are even more important than a will or trust. If something were to happen to your parents (a stroke, coma, dementia) and they hadn't named a power of attorney, someone would have to go through expensive legal proceedings to be appointed to make financial decisions for them so their bills can get paid. And if your parents hadn't spelled out what sort of medical care or end-of-life support they wanted, family members could end up in court fighting over whether to keep them on life support.

These are the type of worst-case scenarios you can avoid if you talk to your parents about the importance of having a power of attorney, advance health care directive, and a will or living trust. It can be a tough discussion to have, though, because it can stir up fears about death. That's why it's important to approach the conversation carefully. Make it clear to your parents that you want to know what their wishes are and that you want to ensure those wishes are legally documented so they can be upheld.

To help you have this conversation, here's what you need to know about the various types of estate planning documents. If your parents tell you that they already have these documents, you still need to discuss with them what legal role they expect you to play. If they have named you as their power of attorney for finances or health care or as the executor of their will, it's a responsibility that you need to take seriously. You will need to discuss what their wishes are so you can fulfill them.

POWER OF ATTORNEY

A power of attorney is a document that gives one or more people the right to make financial decisions[1] for you if you cannot. The power can be broad enough to allow someone to manage all of your financial affairs. Or it can be limited to a specific financial transaction, such closing a real estate deal. It can be springing, which means it will only take effect in certain circumstances – typically, when a person becomes incapacitated. Or it can be effective immediately and durable, which means it's still effective after the person who made it is no longer mentally competent. Of course, this is often the reason someone executes a power of attorney – so someone can make decisions when they are unable to do so. But a power of attorney can be made that would not be effective once mental competency is lost, and it would not be durable.

Elder law attorney Josh Berkley[2] typically recommends that his clients have a general durable power of attorney rather than a limited power of attorney. The problem with the latter is that you don't always know what could come up, and the limits you've placed on your power of attorney could prevent him or her from being able to help make many financial decisions for you. And the problem with a springing power of attorney is that the person who is your agent might not be able to act on your behalf until he or she has jumped through the hoops to prove that you can no longer make decisions on your own – such as getting something in writing from doctors and having those statements notarized. The bigger problem, though, is defining in a springing power of attorney document at what point you are incapacitated. Those triggers that make your power of attorney springing could be subject to argument, Berkley said.

The best bet is to give broad powers to someone you trust. Then if you want the power of attorney to be valid only when something happens to you, "put it someplace safe and have a procedure to get it," Berkley said. Without the actual document, someone who is designated as a power of attorney actually has no power.

That said, here's the most important thing to know about power of attorney: You must be mentally competent to sign a power of attorney document. This means that **this document must be drafted and signed BEFORE your parent has any issue that makes him or her incompetent,** such as a stroke, dementia, or a coma. "The importance of doing it early can't be overstated," Berkely said. "Once something happens to someone, it's too late." Remember Doug Nordman, whom I wrote about in Chapter 4? His father hadn't named a power of attorney before developing Alzheimer's disease, so Doug had to spend more than $10,000 and months going through the legal process to become his dad's conservator. It was the only way at that point he could get the legal authority to manage his father's finances for him.

Not only is going through the conservatorship process expensive, but it takes an emotional toll on families. "It's not something you want to do to your parents – to take them to court to prove they're not competent to handle their affairs," Berkley said. "That's not very pretty to haul Dad in there after having had a stroke or to present enough documents to show he's kind of a potato. Who wants to do that to their parents? Hopefully nobody."

However, it is something you should point out to your parents that could happen if they don't designate someone to be their power of attorney while they are still competent. In this case, a little advance planning can go a long way to preventing big financial headaches down the road. If your parents already have power of attorney documents, find out whether they named you or your siblings as their agents. If they have, ask what the extent of your powers are and where their POA documents are so you can find them when you need to step in and help. Without the original documents, no financial institution or government agency will allow you access to your parents' accounts. Also let your parents know that it would be helpful if they create a list of their financial accounts and other personal information, as outlined in Chapter 9, and tell you how to access it when they can no longer manage their finances on their own.

Questions and concerns your parents might have about power of attorney: If your parents aren't familiar with what a power of attorney is, they might ask questions or have objections to drafting this document. Here are some to expect and ways to respond.

> **Question:** Why do I need to name a power of attorney? My spouse/partner can make decisions for me if I can't.

> **Answer:** Not necessarily. Your spouse or partner will only have access to accounts and property that you hold jointly. In other words, if you have separate bank accounts, your spouse/partner can't access it without power of attorney. Even if you have joint accounts and all of your property is titled in both of your names, your spouse/partner could still run into problems if he/she didn't have power of attorney

but needed to sell that property to pay for your care. Typically, both owners have to sign off on the sale of property. If your spouse/partner wasn't already named your power of attorney, he/she probably couldn't sell the property without your signature.

Plus, what if something such as a car accident happens to both of you? You need a backup – someone else who is designated as power of attorney if neither one of you is able to make financial decisions.

Question: Why should I give someone so much power to do what they want with my money?

Answer: You can give just limited powers. However, attorneys say it's actually better to give broader powers. You just want to make sure you name someone you trust, and that person will be required to act in your best interest. Plus, in most cases, that person won't be able to access any of your financial accounts or make any decisions for you unless he or she has the original power of attorney document signed by you. So you can put it in a safe place and tell your power of attorney how to access it if you reach a point when you can't make decisions on your own.

Question: Why do I even need to worry about this? It will cost me money to go to an attorney to get this document. And I'm sure you'll be able to get access to my accounts to pay my bills if something happens to me.

Answer: Yes, it will cost you money to have an attorney draft a power of attorney document – perhaps a couple hundred dollars to several hundred dollars or more if you also have other estate planning documents drafted. But if you don't have a power of attorney and become unable to make financial decisions on your own, I would have to go to court to become your conservator. That's the only way I could get access to your financial accounts and property. Getting conservatorship requires hiring an attorney and getting doctors to testify that you're incompetent. It could take several months and thousands of dollars to go through that process. I certainly don't want to do that to you, and I'm sure you don't want me to have to go through that.

ADVANCE HEALTH CARE DIRECTIVE

An advance health care directive is a legal form that allows you to spell out what sort of medical care you would or would not want at the end of life (often called a living will).[3] You can identify whether you would want resuscitation by CPR, tube feeding, ventilation, or other treatments to prolong your life. You also can specify whether you would want interventions to manage pain and keep you comfortable at the end of life.

An advance directive also allows you to name someone to make health care decisions for you if you cannot. The document is called a health care power of attorney and the person appointed to make health care decisions is called a health care agent, proxy, or surrogate. To be clear, a health care proxy can only make treatment decisions for you if you are incompetent. However, you must be competent to sign an advance directive.[4] That's why it's important to make sure your parents have this document before a medical emergency or condition leaves them unable to make health care decisions on their own. It allows them to spell out their wishes so there is no confusion about what they want.

Each state has its own statute allowing individuals to make their end-of-life wishes known, said estate planning attorney Elizabeth Sigler.[5] States provide free advance directive forms, which you can download from www.caringinfo.org. For the form to be valid, though, it typically needs to be signed in front of witnesses or adhere to other signing formalities.[6] Also, state forms tend to be too general, according to the American Bar Association.[7] So it can be better to have an attorney draft a more specific or detailed advance directive. If your parents divide their time between two or more states, they should have advance directives for each state, Sigler said.

If your parent does not have an advance health care directive, doctors may consult with you and other family members about what sort of end-of-life care to provide, Sigler said. But problems can arise if family members don't agree on treatment. Sigler had a client whose mother did not have a living will. When she had a stroke that left her in a coma, her children couldn't agree on whether to keep her on life support. So the doctors kept her on life support for seven years until she died. And the financial cost of all those years she was kept on life-prolonging treatment drained all the assets of her estate.

If your parents do have an advance directive, it's important that they give their doctors copies to keep with their medical records. You should also encourage them to discuss with you and other family members what sort of end-of-life care they want and who their health care power of attorney is so there aren't any surprises.

Questions and concerns your parents might have about advance health care directives: The idea of spelling out what sort of care you would or would not want at the end of life can be intimidating. And naming someone to make health care decisions for you is a big decision. So you shouldn't be surprised if your parents have concerns about advance health care directives. Here's how to respond to some potential questions they might have.

> **Question:** Can't I just tell you or my doctor what I want? Why do I need to put something in writing?

> **Answer:** We might not be able to remember what you want when the time comes, and your doctor might also forget. Or you could end up in the hospital and a different doctor will be treating you. Plus, there's no guarantee that any doctor will follow your wishes without a document that spells them out.

> **Question:** I don't even know what sort of end-of-life care I would want. What if I change my mind?

> **Answer:** You should talk with your doctor about your options before deciding and putting anything in

writing. And once you do put something in writing, you can always make changes if you change your mind about the type of care you want.

If you don't make a decision and put it in an advance directive, someone else will have to make a decision for you. If your family members can't decide whether to keep you on life support, it could lead to expensive legal battles in court. Do you want that?

Question: If I name someone to be my health care proxy, does that mean that person can start making decisions for me now?

Answer: No. Your health care proxy can only make decisions about your treatment if you can no longer make your own decisions. However, it's important to talk to your health care proxy about your wishes so there's no confusion. If you don't name someone, then one of us might have to go to court to be appointed your guardian if you can no longer make decisions on your own.[8]

Question: Isn't this just something old people do? I'm not that old yet and am still in good health, so there's no rush to do this.

Answer: You never know what could happen. What if you got in a car accident and we had to decide whether to keep you on life support? We wouldn't feel comfortable making that decision for you.

A WILL OR LIVING TRUST

A **will** is a legal document lets you spell out who gets what when you die. Wills aren't just for the rich and famous. Even if you don't have a lot, you still probably want to have a say in what happens to your property. But if you die without a will, your state's laws will dictate who gets what, said estate planning attorney Liza Hanks.[9] That means your house, your car, or any money you have in the bank might go to someone you don't want to have it. It also could lead to family feuds.

You can point this out when talking to your parents about why they need to have wills. You might also want to let your parents know that having a will is like a gift to you, your siblings, and other family members because you won't have to make difficult decisions at a time when you're grieving.

A will also allows you to name an executor – someone who will act on your behalf after you die. This person will be responsible for filing your last tax return, settling debts, and distributing your assets. "Each state's statutes have restrictions on who can serve as an executor," Sigler said. For example, the person typically needs to be at least 18 years old. And some states require that the executor be a resident of that state. Some allow nonresidents to be executors as long as they are related to the decedent. However, a co-executor who is a state resident might need to be named. This is something to keep in mind if you don't live in the same state or country as your parents and they want to name you as their executor. If you aren't able to travel to handle duties as an executor or your parents' state doesn't allow nonresidents to be named executors, they should consider naming another relative, a family friend, or professional such as an attorney, bank, or trust company, Sigler said.

The executor must be able to participate in the probate process, which is the legal process of distributing property.[10] Insurance policies and some retirement accounts can bypass the probate process as long as beneficiaries are named,[11] which is why it's important to keep beneficiaries on those accounts updated. And accounts designated as payable on death can be transferred to beneficiaries without going through probate.

The length of probate varies by state, but, on average, it takes six to nine months, according to the American Bar Association.[12] The cost of court fees and attorney fees associated with probate also varies by state. In some states, such as California where Hanks is an attorney, the cost of probate can be very high because attorneys can charge a fee that is a percentage of the estate going through probate. For example, the attorney's fee for a $1 million estate (which isn't outrageous in California because home values are so high) would be $23,000, Hanks said. Probate and that high fee could be avoided with a living trust.

A **living trust** is similar to a will because it lets you specify how you want your assets distributed when you die. But it can be much more detailed than a will about how and when beneficiaries will get assets. The biggest difference, though, is that assets in a living trust avoid probate. In a state such as California, that can mean big savings for people with large estates. Hanks said attorneys charge $3,000 to $5,000 for a living trust, which is much more than a will but a fraction of the cost of probate.

However, as I said, assets *in* a living trust avoid probate. That means your assets have to be transferred to the trust while you're alive. Assets with designated beneficiaries such as life insurance policies, retirement accounts, and payable-on-death accounts don't have to be transferred to a living trust because they will automatically go to beneficiaries when you die. But you have to transfer investment accounts, your property such as your house, and any other valuable assets. That can involve changing the title on deeds from your name to the trust and filling out forms with financial institutions. You also have to name a trustee to manage the assets in the trust. You can name yourself to be trustee, then name a successor trustee to manage the trust once you die.

In addition to avoiding probate, having a living trust can protect privacy. A will becomes public record when it goes through probate. A living trust, on the other hand, is never made public. It can be worth the time, money, and effort to create and fund a living trust for people with large estates, those who want to protect their privacy, or those who want to have more control over their assets after they die, Berkley said. But your parents shouldn't pay more to create a trust just to avoid probate if they live in a state where the cost of probate isn't high, he said.

If your parents have wills, living trusts, or both, you need to ask where those documents are stored. These documents won't do any good if no one can find them. Also ask whom they have named to be executor or trustee. If it's you, consider whether it's a job you're equipped to handle. It can be incredibly time consuming, demand a lot of attention to detail, and require that you be able to get along with other beneficiaries. To make the task easier for you, ask that your parents create a detailed list of their property and accounts and store that list with their will so you won't have to play detective when they die.

Questions and concerns your parents might have about wills and living trusts: Less than half of adults have a will or trust, according to a survey by Caring.com. If your parents are among the majority of Americans who don't have one of these important legal documents, it could be because they don't recognize how important they are. It also could be because they don't want to have to think about their death, or just simply haven't gotten around to writing a will. Regardless, you might face some resistance from them if you bring up the topic of wills and living trusts. Here are some questions they might ask as well as ways you can respond.

> **Question:** Why do I need a will? Your mom/dad will just get everything when I die.
>
> > **Answer:** That depends. Some states may divide property between the surviving spouse and children or other relatives if you don't have a will that specifies who gets what. So mom/dad might not get everything. It would probably be a good idea to meet with an attorney to find out what the law is in your state and to have a will drafted if you want control over where your property goes.
>
> **Question:** Why do I need a will? I'm not rich.
>
> > **Answer:** Even if you don't have much, you still probably want a say in who gets what. If you don't have a will, a judge will decide who gets your property. It might end up going to someone you don't want to get it.
>
> **Question:** Can't I just write my will out by hand? Do I really need to hire an attorney?
>
> > **Answer:** You can write your own will, but you have to do it entirely by hand, sign it, and date it. But it might not stand up in court as well as a will drafted by an attorney. Also, it might not cover all of the bases you

need it to cover because you're not an attorney and don't have experience writing wills.

Question: My attorney says I should have a living trust to avoid probate. Is that a good idea?

Answer: You should ask your attorney why probate is so bad. If he says it will be expensive, ask him or her much it will cost. A living trust could be right for you, but it could also be a way for the attorney to make more money if he or she charges a lot more for a living trust than a will.

Concern: I don't want to talk about this because it makes me think about death.

Response: I know this is difficult for you. It's difficult for me to think about something happening to you. But it will be even more difficult for us to make decisions about who gets what if you don't have a will. We want to make sure to uphold your wishes, but that means we have to know what they are. (You could even tell your parent that writing a will could help prevent family arguments because his or her wishes will be known.)

SHOULD YOUR PARENTS GO THE DIY ROUTE?

Ideally, your parents should work with an attorney to draft these estate planning documents to ensure that they adhere to state laws and meet your parents' needs. They can find an estate planning attorney by contacting their state bar association or by getting referrals from friends or family.

If your parents can't afford to hire an attorney, there are free and low-cost ways for them to get the legal documents they need. For example, state bar associations offer free, downloadable will forms. State advance health care directive forms can be downloaded from www.caringinfo.org. State agencies offer free power of attorney forms that can be found by searching the state name and "power of attorney form." Your parents also can get low-cost estate planning documents at websites such as Nolo.com, LegalZoom.com, and RocketLawyer.com.

Be aware that these no- and low-cost options are made to be general and are not personalized, said Hanks, who is an author for Nolo[13] in addition to being an estate planning attorney. But basic is better than nothing, she said. Your parents could upgrade these documents later if their finances improve or when they have more time to meet with an attorney. Keep in mind, though, that these documents need to be properly signed to be valid. And they might not hold up to challenges in court as well as attorney-drafted documents.

NOTES

1. American Bar Association (2015), "Power of Attorney," https://www .americanbar.org/groups/real_property_trust_estate/resources/estate_ planning/power_of_attorney/ (Accessed Jan. 3, 2019).
2. Josh Berkley, https://www.berkleyoliver.com/About/ (Accessed Jan. 3, 2019).
3. National Institute on Aging, "Advance Care Planning: Healthcare Directives," https://www.nia.nih.gov/health/advance-care-planning-healthcare-directives (Accessed Jan. 3, 2019).
4. American Bar Association (2012), "Law for Older Americans," https:// www.americanbar.org/groups/public_education/resources/law_issues_ for_consumers/directive_whatis/ (Accessed Jan. 3, 2019).
5. Elizabeth Sigler, https://www.boamlaw.com/attorney/elizabeth-w-sigler/ (Accessed Jan. 3, 2019).
6. American Bar Association, "Myths and Facts About Health Care Advance Directives," https://www.americanbar.org/content/dam/aba/migrated/ Commissions/myths_fact_hc_ad.authcheckdam.pdf (Accessed Jan. 3, 2019).
7. American Bar Association, "Myths and Facts About Health Care Advance Directives," https://www.americanbar.org/content/dam/aba/migrated/ Commissions/myths_fact_hc_ad.authcheckdam.pdf (Accessed Jan. 3, 2019).
8. American Bar Association, "Myths and Facts About Health Care Advance Directives," https://www.americanbar.org/content/dam/aba/migrated/ Commissions/myths_fact_hc_ad.authcheckdam.pdf (Accessed Jan. 3, 2019).

9. Liza Hanks, https://www.lizahanks.com/ (Accessed Jan. 3, 2019).
10. American Bar Association (2013), "Wills and Estates: The Probate Process," https://www.americanbar.org/groups/public_education/resources /law_issues_for_consumers/probate/ (Accessed Jan. 3, 2019).
11. Brette Sember, "Do All Wills Need to Go Through Probate?" LegalZoom, https://www.legalzoom.com/articles/do-all-wills-need-to-go-through-probate (Accessed Jan. 3, 2019).
12. American Bar Association (2012), "Wills and Estates: The Probate Process," https://www.americanbar.org/groups/public_education/resources /law_issues_for_consumers/probate/.
13. Liza Hanks, https://www.linkedin.com/in/lizahanks/ (Accessed Jan. 3, 2019).

Talking to Your Parents About Scammers

Shortly after her father died, Rita Cheng gave her mom a smartphone to make it easier for her to keep in touch with friends. It seemed like the right thing to do, she said. But it opened up opportunities for her mom to start connecting with people on Facebook and on websites – people who weren't always who they said they were.

Rita's mom started spending a lot of time on her phone and talking about a guy named Bill. This set off an internal alarm for Rita, who is a certified financial planner, CEO of Blue Ocean Global Wealth, and member of an elder abuse prevention committee in Washington, D.C.[1] She wanted her mom to make friends and didn't want to poke around in her business too much. But she started asking questions and warning her mom about the dangers of dating in the digital world. Rita told her mom not to invite people she had met online to her home and to meet only during the day – never at night – and only in a public place.

However, her mom was vulnerable after the death of Rita's dad, and the man she had been talking to online took advantage of that. He had persuaded her to transfer $15,000 to a bank account so he could buy plane tickets for them and they could take a trip together. If it weren't for a bizarre set of events, Rita might not have found out that her mom had been scammed soon enough to take action.

A social worker in Maryland where Rita's mom lives called Rita to tell her that her mom was a victim of a sweetheart scam.

"I started crying because I thought, 'How could I let this happen?'" Rita said.

The Maryland social worker had gotten a call from a social worker in Portland, Oregon, who had been called by a woman who said she had a lot of money in her bank account but didn't want it because it would've made her ineligible for the Social Security disability benefits she was receiving. The money had been transferred to the account by Rita's mom. Rita suspects that the person who befriended her mom online had used the Oregon woman's account number for the transfer.

The social worker had called Rita's mom to get more information about the money transfer and figured out she had been scammed. Rita's mom then asked the social worker to call Rita, who then spent the next six months calling and writing the bank in Oregon to get back her mom's money. After jumping through several hoops, Rita finally recovered $13,600 of the $15,000 that her mom thought she was sending to a guy named Bill to pay for a vacation for them.

Cheng's mother was just one of thousands of older adults who become victims of online sweetheart scams every year. In 2017, the FBI's Internet Crime Complaint Center received 15,372 complaints about romance scams that cost victims more than $211 million. Unfortunately, this isn't the only way scammers are targeting older adults.

About 1 in 20 older Americans have reported being victims of financial exploitation, according to the National Adult Protective Services Association (NAPSA).[2] But that number likely doesn't represent the true scope of the problem because only one in 44 cases of financial abuse is reported, according to NAPSA. Although the total amount of money older adults lose every year to fraud isn't known, some estimates show that it's in the billions of dollars.[3]

In short, financial exploitation of older adults is a big problem. If you don't want your parents to become part of the statistics, you need to make them aware of the ways scammers could target them so they don't become victims.

WHY OLDER ADULTS ARE TARGETS

Anyone can become a victim of a scam or fraud. However, older adults are especially susceptible for several reasons. You don't need to share all of these reasons with your parents, but it's important for you to know why they are targets.

Scammers think they have money. One of the primary reasons con artists prey on older adults is because they assume they have a stash of retirement savings, a stream of income from Social Security, and a pension or other assets. "They're being targeted because that's where scammers think the money is," said Kathy Stokes,[4] a fraud expert for AARP, the nation's leading advocacy group for adults ages 50 and older.

Scammers assume they're vulnerable. A decline in physical and mental health can make older adults more susceptible to financial exploitation. A New York State study[5] of financial exploitation among the elderly found that 68 percent of alleged victims in that state had at least one serious health impairment. And 58 percent were adults who required help with at least one daily activity, such as transportation and meal preparation.

It's not just health issues that make older adults vulnerable. Inevitably, financial decision-making abilities decline with age, according to the National Endowment for Financial Education. So even healthy adults can become fraud victims because it may become more difficult for them to manage their money and recognize financial risks as they age.

Scammers know they're trusting. Your parent's generation was raised to be polite and respectful – and scammers exploit these traits. According to the FBI, con artists know that older adults are less likely to hang up when they call or say no to their requests.

Scammers know they probably won't report the crime. Older adults are less likely to report that they're victims of fraud because they don't realize they've been scammed, are too embarrassed, or don't know how to report the crime, according to the FBI. Even if older adults actually report that they've been victimized, scammers aren't too worried they'll get caught. That's because scammers expect their victims' age to make it difficult for them to remember details of the crime, according to the FBI.

Unfortunately, many of the scammers who are exploiting older adults aren't strangers to them. They're family members. Various studies[6] have found that in one-third to two-thirds of cases of financial exploitation, the perpetrators were family members. They take advantage of aging adults' trust and their roles as caregivers to line their own pockets. That's why it's important to warn your parents not only about strangers who want to take advantage of them but also about people who are close to them who might take advantage of their generosity. *Above all, you shouldn't betray your parents' trust.*

HOW TO HELP PROTECT YOUR PARENTS FROM EXPLOITATION

No matter what you do, you can't guarantee that your parents won't become victims of financial exploitation. But you can help lower their risk by talking to them about scams and fraud. Plus, these discussions might open the door to more conversations about your parents' finances and help you work together to protect their money. Here's how to get started, what you should say, and steps you can take to reduce their risk of becoming victims.

Use examples to start the conversation. One of the best ways to start talking to your parents about scams is to use an example, Stokes said. It can be an article you read or a report you heard on the radio or TV news. Better yet, you could mention that you got a phone call from a scammer and wanted to warn your parents to be on the lookout.

Financial planner John Cooper said he actually clips newspaper articles about the latest scams and gives them to clients. If you get all of your news online, he recommends actively searching for articles, then emailing them to your parents – or printing them out if they don't use email. You can find detailed information about the various types of scams on the Better Business Bureau's website at www.bbb.org/scamtips. The AARP

Fraud Watch Network (www.aarp.org/fraudwatchnetwork) also has fraud news and useful information on spotting and avoiding scams. You can also use the resources on these sites to educate yourself about scams before talking to your parents.

Explain why they are at risk. After you warn your parents about scams you've heard about, let them know why they're likely to be targets. However, DO NOT tell them it's because they're old or vulnerable. You don't need to list all of the reasons I mentioned that older adults are more likely to be exploited. Instead, focus on the primary reason. "Explain to them that it's their age group that is a prime target for scammers because they're perceived to have a bucket of retirement savings or a stream of income from pensions or Social Security or other assets," Stokes said.

Alert your parents to red flags. You can't just tell your parents to hang up on scammers when they call, throw away solicitations that come in the mail, or avoid clicking on links in suspicious emails and expect that to keep them safe. Instead, you need to talk with them about the tactics scammers use so they can identify when someone might be trying to con them. "Ask them if they can find their inner skeptic any time a stranger calls or emails or comes to the door," Stokes said. "They taught us never to talk to strangers. So we're just reminding them the great rule they taught us when we were growing up." Then tell your parents to watch out for these red flags:

- Fees to collect winnings: If your parents get a call that they've won the lottery or a sweepstakes and have to pay a fee to collect their winnings, it's probably a scam. For starters, if they didn't enter a sweepstakes or buy a lottery ticket, there's no way they could win. Plus, you never have to pay fees to collect lottery winnings, Stokes said. That's just the way scammers get you to part with your money. In fact, any request to wire money is a big red flag.
- Calls from government agencies: If your parents get a call from someone claiming to be with the IRS and stating that they owe money, it's a scam. The same goes for calls from someone claiming to be with the

Social Security Administration, Medicare, Federal Trade Commission, or other government agency. "People are pretending to be from these agencies to get at your personal information or your money," Stokes said. Let your parents know that government agencies will not call them unless your parents expect them to call based on an issue they are already aware of, nor will they send emails. These agencies communicate by mail and will only contact you by phone if you call them first and have to leave a message requesting a return call. And they will never ask you to pay by wiring money.[7]

- Emergency calls from the grandkids: Clearly, a call from the grandkids shouldn't send up a red flag. But warn your parents that if they get a call from someone claiming to be their grandchild in trouble and in desperate need of cash fast, it could be a scam. Telltale signs include a plea not to tell Mom or Dad and a request to wire money, Stokes said. If they get a call like this, tell your parents to ask the caller questions that only their grandchild could answer. Or they could tell the person they need to switch phones and call right back – then call the grandchild's number (not a number the caller gives you).

- Unsolicited calls: Let your parents know that any time they get a call from someone they don't know or a group they've never had contact with that is asking for personal information, it's a big red flag. If your parents are worried that it might be a legitimate request for information, they could hang up then look up the number for the agency, office, or organization that supposedly is calling and call it directly to see if it was trying to contact them.

- Limited-time offers: Warn your parents to watch out for emails, text messages, or even phone calls from people offering them a chance to get in on a money-making opportunity or investment for a limited time only. Also, these pitches tend to include language that this so-called deal is only being offered to a select group of people. "Anyone who calls or sends a letter and says there's an amazing opportunity for an investment but it's only available to the 52 people we've identified we want to offer it to, it's not legitimate," Stokes said. Scammers and unscrupulous investment brokers want people to feel like they're special and to act quickly without doing any research.

- High-pressure sales tactics: Let your parents know that it's a red flag if someone who is trying to sell them something becomes aggressive or threatening. High-pressure sales tactics are meant to force people into snap decisions and often are a sign of a con, according to the Better Business Bureau.[8]
- Free lunches: There's a good chance your parents will get offers in the mail to attend free lunch or free dinner investment seminars. You should warn them that these seminars are sales pitches[9] meant to get people to purchase high-fee, unsuitable, or even fraudulent investments. And the sales people use high-pressure tactics to try to seal the deal. "My advice: There is no free lunch," Stokes said. "Don't go."
- High-return investments with no risks: A pitch for an investment that offers high returns with no risk might sound ideal to your parents – especially if they're trying to boost their retirement savings. But let them know that all investments have some level of risk.[10] Typically, the higher the return, the more risk you have to take.

You can visit CameronHuddleston.com for a full list of scam red flags and examples of common scams to download, print, and share with your parents.

Don't just tell them to hang up. Instead, create a refusal script. There are so many ways scammers can reach victims now, but the primary way is still the telephone, Stokes said. But you can't just tell your parents not to answer the phone if caller ID shows a number they don't recognize or to hang up if it's someone they don't know. "It's not in their DNA," Stokes said. They think it's rude not to answer or to hang up. And they might worry that if they don't answer it, they might miss an important call.

So you need to help them come up with a sentence that helps them get off the phone without feeling bad. Stokes said she told her mom to tell telemarketers and questionable callers that she's having tea with Officer Brady and couldn't take the call. You could tell your parents to say something similar, or even "I'm on the way out the door."

Also caution your parents against staying on the phone with scammers if they know it's a con but just want to mess with the person. Stokes said that phone numbers are bought and sold, and scammers look at call data to see how long people stay on the line. "If you're going to stay on the phone for five minutes because you're screwing with the person who's trying to scam you, you're a hot commodity," Stokes said. "That number is going to be bought and sold a zillion times. And you're going to be on more lists. So it's not a good idea to engage."

And those robo-calls that give the option to opt out of future calls by pressing a number are a ploy. "You press that number, and now you're on the list because they know it's a hot number," Stokes said. So warn your parents to watch out for this trick.

Help your parents avoid telemarketing and spam calls. Your parents can register their home and mobile phone numbers for free with the National Do Not Call Registry at donotcall .gov or 1-888-382-1222 to stop unwanted sales calls. This does not stop political, charitable, survey, or debt collection calls. And it doesn't prevent scammers from calling – only legitimate telemarketing companies. But because it will prevent legitimate companies from calling, your parents will know that the calls they still are getting are likely from scammers.

Your parents might be able to block anonymous calls to their landline (depending on their service provider) by picking up the phone and dialing *77.[11] To remove the block, dial *87. They can download a free mobile app such as Hiya to help identify and limit spam calls to their cell phones, or contact their cell phone service provider to see what call blocking options it provides.

Warn them about unscrupulous financial professionals and risky investments. Just because someone is a financial professional doesn't mean that person will act ethically. That's why it's important to talk with your parents about the importance of working with a financial professional who will work in their best interest. Most, if not all, will claim that they work in the clients' best interest, but only those who are fiduciaries are required by law to do so. Fiduciaries are advisers who typically operate on fee-only or fee-based (fee and commission) compensation and include Registered Investment Advisers (RIAs)[12] and Certified Financial Planners (CFPs).[13] Non-fiduciaries such as brokers and insurance agents can be paid by commission on the products they sell and must adhere to a suitability standard, which requires them to make suitable recommendations but doesn't require them to put clients' interests above theirs. You can help your parents check the background of financial professionals with the Financial Industry Regulatory Authority's BrokerCheck at www.finra.org.

Regardless of whether the financial professionals your parents work with are fiduciaries or non-fiduciaries, you should encourage them to ask questions such as what licenses they hold, whether any disciplinary actions have been taken against them, how they get paid, and whether they can provide references. If the professionals can't provide clear answers, that should raise a red flag. AARP has a sample script and questions your parents can use when meeting with a financial professional at www.aarp.org/interviewanadvisor.

Also alert your parents to investment fraud red flags such as a promise of guaranteed high returns with no risk, complex investing techniques that the professional can't clearly explain, or securities that aren't registered or don't have documentation that can be reviewed for more information.[14] The Securities and Exchange Commission provides detailed information about investments that are marketed to seniors and how to avoid fraud at www.investor.gov/seniors.

Help them monitor their financial accounts. Recommend to your parents that they set up online access for all of their financial accounts if they haven't already. They might balk because they think it's risky. But it's actually riskier if they don't have online access to their accounts, Stokes said. "When you have that access, you can regularly see what's going on in those accounts and identify fraud," she said. "If you don't set up electronic access to your account, a scammer potentially can have the only electronic access to that account."

AARP has received reports of scammers who have used other adults' personal information to create online Social Security accounts because the victims hadn't already set up accounts. Then the thieves steal benefits by changing bank routing numbers for deposits. You can help your parents set up a "my Social Security" account by going to www.SSA.gov/myaccount. Not only will this prevent thieves from setting up accounts in your parents' names, but also it will allow them to keep tabs on their benefits and see how much they will get if they aren't already collecting Social Security.

Be sure to caution your parents to use different and strong passwords with a mixture of upper- and lowercase letters, numbers, and symbols for each of their online accounts. They could create a list of those passwords (and stash it someplace safe) or use an online password manager program such as Dashlane, which also generates strong passwords for users. It has both free and paid versions.

Also encourage your parents to set up alerts on their bank and credit card accounts (or help them do it). Most financial institutions allow account holders to sign up to receive text or email messages to be notified of activity on their accounts. These alerts will help your parents identify fraudulent use of their cards immediately if they see that there are transactions that they haven't made. It only takes a few minutes to log onto online bank and credit card accounts to set up these alerts.

Help them check their credit reports. Your parents could already be victims of fraud and not even know. One way to find out is to have them check their credit reports, which will show all of the lines of credit opened in their names. If they've been victims of identity theft, there might be accounts in their names that they didn't open.

Consumers are entitled to a free copy of their credit report every year from each of the three credit bureaus – Experian, Equifax, and TransUnion. These reports are available at www.annualcreditreport.com. You can offer to help your parents download their reports from the site and check them for wrong amounts on accounts or for accounts they didn't open.

If they find suspicious accounts, tell them to contact the credit bureaus using the phone numbers listed on their credit reports and ask for the fraud departments, which can help walk them through the steps they need to take. They also need to contact the creditors to let them know that fraudulent accounts were created in their names. And report to local law enforcement that their identities were stolen. They should ask for a copy of the police incident report because they might need it when disputing fraudulent accounts. Your parents also should put a credit freeze on their credit reports with all three bureaus. This prevents thieves from opening accounts in their names because lenders can't authorize new lines of credit without seeing their credit reports first. The can put a credit freeze on their reports for free (and lift the freeze if they want to apply for credit) by visiting the websites or calling the three credit bureaus.

- Equifax: https://www.equifax.com/personal/credit-report-services/ or 1-800-685-1111
- Experian: https://www.experian.com/freeze/center.html or 1-888-397-3742
- TransUnion: https://www.transunion.com/credit-freeze or 1-888-909-8872

Point them to resources. Plenty of resources online offer a wealth of information about how older adults can protect themselves from financial exploitation. You could point your parents to these resources or print the information for them if they're not comfortable using the Internet.

- National Adult Protective Services Association: http://www.napsa-now.org/
- AARP Fraud Watch Network: www.aarp.org/fraudwatch network
- Consumer Financial Protection Bureau http://www.consumerfinance.gov
- Federal Trade Commission Scam Alerts https://www.consumer.ftc.gov/features/scam-alerts
- Security and Exchange Commission's "A Guide for Seniors" https://www.sec.gov/investor/seniors/guidefor seniors.pdf

- Better Business Bureau Scam Tips: https://www.bbb.org/ scamtips
- Protect Seniors Online: https://www.protectseniors online.com/

WARNING SIGNS YOUR PARENTS ARE VICTIMS

Because older adults don't always realize they've been scammed or can be too ashamed to admit it, you need to keep an eye out for signs that your parents are being financially exploited. You might have to play detective by snooping a little to find clues. And you need to be ready to step in if you discover that they have been scammed. As Rita realized after learning that her mom had been exploited, she had to get involved to help her mom recover her money. And she had more talks with her mom about how to protect herself from con artists, which paid off when her mom recognized that someone was trying to pull the grandparent scam on her. "We tell our children not to talk to strangers," Rita said. "We need to do the same with our parents. We need to keep our parents safe."

With that in mind, look for these red flags that your parents are being financially exploited.

- Changes in spending patterns: Be wary if your parents once were flush with cash but now are talking about how they barely have enough to get by. It could be that they didn't plan well for retirement and now are struggling to meet ends meet. But it could be a sign that they've lost a lot of money to a scam.
- Offering personal information over the phone: When visiting with your parents, pay attention to the sort of information they share over the phone. If they get calls and you hear them giving out personal details such as birthdates, Social Security numbers, and credit card numbers, they likely are setting themselves up to be scam victims.
- Lots of sweepstakes forms and donation requests in your parents' mail: Chances are your parents already have entered sweepstakes or made contributions to various groups if they're getting lots of these types of letters in the

mail. That's because their past participation or donations has helped them land on junk mail lists – which means the solicitations will keep coming. Suggest that they go to DMAchoice.org to opt out of direct mail from legitimate groups. Then they'll know that offers, entry forms, and donation requests they're still getting truly are junk mail that can be tossed. You could also help your parents research legitimate charities at www.charitynavigator.org and come up with a list of organizations they want to help. Then they could develop a giving plan for those groups only.

- Debt collection notices or bills from unknown lenders: Don't dismiss comments or complaints from your parents that they're getting bills for accounts they didn't open or debt collection notices for amounts they don't owe. This is likely a sign that their identity has been stolen and has been used to open accounts in their name.

- Unnecessary home repairs: Lately, your parents always seem to be making one repair or another to their home. But if it's in good condition and the repairs seem unnecessary, it might mean that they've been conned by a contractor.

- Unnecessary medical equipment or tests: If your relatively healthy parents start getting lots of medical tests or now have medical equipment they don't seem to need, it could be a sign of health care fraud. Con artists will offer free medical screenings and supplies in exchange for patients' health insurance information – which is then stolen and used fraudulently, according to the FBI.[15]

- Investments that sound too good to be true: If your parents start talking about new investments they recently made that are guaranteed to double in value or have absolutely no risk, press them for more details. There's a good chance they've been conned into buying a fraudulent investment and might need help getting out of it before they lose any more money.

- A new friend in your parent's life: If your single parent meets someone, you might be happy that he or she is no longer sitting at home alone. But be wary if your parent starts telling you that his or her new friend has asked for financial help or has done anything else that sounds suspicious. Your parent could be a victim of a sweetheart scam.

If you do suspect that your parents are victims, don't make a bad situation worse by blaming them. "If you're a victim of a scam and lose money over the phone, how different is it from being pickpocketed or being held at a gunpoint? There are bad guys doing bad things," Stokes said. "It's not the victim's fault."

Instead offer to help your parents repair the damage and avoid further financial losses by reporting the crime, putting a freeze on their credit reports, contacting their bank, calling creditors to close fraudulent accounts, changing account passwords, and getting a new license if theirs is stolen.

HOW TO PROTECT PARENTS WITH DEMENTIA FROM SCAMS

If your parents already have dementia or a health condition that has affected their reasoning, you can't just warn them about red flags. You have to take an active role in reducing their risk of becoming scam victims. That's because they won't remember your instructions. Even if they do, they likely won't be able to act on them because of their cognitive decline.

I saw this firsthand with my mom. In the early stages of her dementia while she still was living alone, she would receive several donation requests and sweepstakes entry forms in the mail every day. They were hitting her up for money, which she was readily handing over to many of these groups. I remember one, in particular, that sent donation requests practically every month. It was a boarding school in South Dakota that had a name similar to the Catholic school where she had taught preschool in Kentucky. She had no connection to the South Dakota school and likely was confused by the similar name – which prompted her to respond to all of the donation requests she got with checks.

I stepped in by going through her mail daily to intercept all of the donation requests and sweepstakes forms she was getting. I left her with her checkbook so she had a way to pay for things (she didn't use a debit card). But I took away her credit cards so she couldn't hand out that information over the phone. I also set up online banking for her so I could monitor her account to make sure she wasn't writing checks to scammers.

Even those efforts weren't enough to protect her, though. She was almost swindled out of hundreds of dollars by a phone scammer who had persuaded her she had won a sweepstakes and needed to wire money to collect her prize. My mom called my uncle to ask him how to wire money. He immediately knew it was a scam and called me to tell me what was going on. I rushed to my mom's house to discover her on the phone with the scammer. I asked if I could talk to the person, then told him not to call back. Of course, he did call back. And despite my attempts to explain to my mom what was going on, she was convinced that she had hit the jackpot and needed to send money to collect her winnings. There was no reasoning with her. So I stayed with her that day to intercept the calls. Finally, the scammer got the clue and stopped.

That event was a big wake-up call for me. I realized my mom couldn't be left alone anymore because she was going to become a victim. I couldn't risk letting her lose all of her money to con artists. So I hired someone to stay with her during the day. I then moved her in with me to keep an even closer eye on her and helped her as her Alzheimer's progressed. In the next two chapters, I'll walk you through how to have conversations with your parents about long-term care and when it's time for them to move.

NOTES

1. Marguerita (Rita) Cheng, https://www.linkedin.com/in/marguerita cheng/ (Accessed Jan. 3, 2019).
2. National Adult Protective Services Administration, "Elder Financial Exploitation," http://www.napsa-now.org/policy-advocacy/exploitation/ (Accessed Jan. 3, 2019).

3. Securities and Exchange Commission Office of the Investor Advocate (2018), "Elder Financial Exploitation: Why It Is a Concern, What Regulators Are Doing About It, and Looking Ahead," https://www.sec.gov/files/elder-financial-exploitation.pdf (Accessed Jan. 3, 2019).

4. Kathy Stokes, https://www.linkedin.com/in/kathy-stokes-9920032/ (Accessed Jan. 3, 2019).

5. New York State Office of Children and Family Services (2016), "The New York State Cost of Financial Exploitation Study," https://ocfs.ny.gov/main/reports/Cost%20of%20Financial%20Exploitation%20Study%20FINAL%20May%202016.pdf (Accessed Jan. 3, 2019).

6. New York State Office of Children and Family Services, (2016), "The New York State Cost of Financial Exploitation Study," https://ocfs.ny.gov/main/reports/Cost%20of%20Financial%20Exploitation%20Study%20FINAL%20May%202016.pdf; National Center on Elder Abuse, https://ncea.acl.gov/whatwedo/research/statistics.html; Stacey Wood and Peter A. Lichtenberg (2016), "Financial Capacity and Financial Exploitation of Older Adults: Research Findings, Policy Recommendations and Clinical Implications," National Institutes of Health, https://www.ncbi.nlm.nih.gov/pmc/articles/PMC5463983/ (Accessed Jan. 3, 2019).

7. Alvaro Puig (2015), "Avoiding Money Wiring Scams," Federal Trade Commission, https://www.consumer.ftc.gov/blog/2015/08/avoiding-money-wiring-scams (Accessed Jan. 3, 2019).

8. Better Business Bureau, "10 Red Flags You Are Being Scammed," https://www.bbb.org/us/storage/158/documents/press%20releases/RedFlags201.pdf (Accessed Jan. 3, 2019).

9. FINRA Investor Education Foundation, "How to Recognize a Free Lunch Investment Seminar Scam," https://www.saveandinvest.org/video/recognize-free-lunch-investment-seminar-scam (Accessed Jan. 3, 2019).

10. Financial Industry Regulatory Authority, "Red Flags of Fraud," http://www.finra.org/investors/red-flags-fraud (Accessed Jan. 3, 2019).

11. AT&T Community Forums, (2017), "Anonymous Call Rejection (*77) – Traditional Landline," https://forums.att.com/t5/AT-T-Phone-Features/Anonymous-Call-Rejection-77-Traditional-Landline/td-p/5137752 (Accessed Jan. 3, 2019).

12. Financial Industry Regulatory Authority, "Investment Advisers," http://www.finra.org/investors/investment-advisers; Will Kenton, (2018), "Registered Investment Advisor," Investopedia, https://www.investopedia.com/terms/r/ria.asp (Accessed Jan. 3, 2019).

13. Certified Financial Planner Board of Standards, "CFP Certification Requirements," https://www.cfp.net/become-a-cfp-professional/cfp-cer tification-requirements (Accessed Jan. 3, 2019).

14. Financial Industry Regulatory Authority, "Red Flags of Fraud," http:// www.finra.org/investors/red-flags-fraud (Accessed Jan. 3, 2019).

15. Federal Bureau of Investigation, "Health Care Fraud," https://www.fbi .gov/investigate/white-collar-crime/health-care-fraud (Accessed Jan. 3, 2019).

12

Talking to Your Parents About Long-Term Care

Talking to your parents about long-term care might be one of the most difficult conversations you can have. Let's face it: None of us likes to think about the possibility that we will have to rely on someone else to take care of us someday. It's even harder to stomach the idea of ending up in a nursing home. In fact, a 2018 survey by Nationwide Retirement Institute found that 56 percent of respondents would rather die than live in a nursing home.[1]

Yet, here I am saying that you should talk to your parents about something they might find even worse than death. Why? Because I've learned from experience that the sooner you start talking about long-term care, the more time you'll have to plan for it and the easier it will be to keep emotions out of the conversation.

By having conversations with your parents about long-term care well before there is a need for it, you're talking in hypothetical terms. "If something happens, do you have a plan . . ." When Mom is already losing her memory or Dad has had a stroke and needs round-the-clock care, the conversation shifts from "If this happens" to "How are we going to handle this?" The chance to have a rational discussion is most likely gone now that everyone is in crisis mode.

I know what you're thinking, though. Why even bother talking about something that might never happen? Let me throw out a few facts and figures for you to consider:

- About 70 percent of adults 65 and older will need long-term care at some point.[2]
- The average length of long-term care for those who need it is 3.9 years.[3]
- Women are more likely to need a high level of care – 4.4 years versus 3.2 years for men.[4]
- More than a quarter of Americans turning 65 will have long-term care costs of at least $100,000; 15 percent will have costs that exceed $250,000.[5]
- Medicare does not pay for most long-term care services – typically just short-term care in a nursing facility after hospitalization.[6]

As you can see, the odds that your parents will need long-term care are pretty high. If they need care, the cost can be *extremely* high. Professional care can range from about $4,000 a month for a home health aide or assisted living to more than $8,000 a month for a private room in a skilled nursing facility, according to figures from the 2018 Genworth Cost of Care Survey.[7] The problem is, most Americans – perhaps even your parents – aren't prepared to pay for this cost. As I pointed out, Medicare typically does not cover long-term care. The same goes for health insurance.[8] Long-term care insurance is available, but only 11 percent of adults have it, according to the Bipartisan Policy Center.[9] As a result, most people who need long-term care end up relying on family or friends to help. That means **you could be your parents long-term care plan**.

Before you say, "Of course I'll help care for my parents," you need to understand what it entails. For starters, caregiving can be a full-time job. I know this from my own experience with my mom, who has Alzheimer's disease. An Associated Press-NORC Center for Public Affairs Research study[10] also found that the amount of time about a quarter of caregivers spend each week providing care is equivalent to a full-time job. Here are some more statistics from that study, which show what an undertaking being a caregiver really is.

- Eight in 10 caregivers pay for costs out of their own pockets, with 13 percent spending $500 or more a month.
- 43 percent of caregivers have dipped into their savings, and 23 percent have reduced how much they saved for retirement.
- 39 percent of caregivers have a health problem, and 40 percent say it's harder to manage their own health as a result of caregiving.

In short, being a caregiver can take a serious toll on your finances and your health. If you have children of your own, you need to consider what the ripple effects of caring for a parent will have on them. I'm not sharing all of these statistics to scare you; well okay, maybe a little. But I want you to be armed with facts that you can share with your parents as you discuss the need to plan for long-term care. These facts also can inform your decision about how much help you're willing and able to provide your parents.

WHAT LONG-TERM CARE IS

The standard definition of long-term care[11] is a range of services to help people with the basic activities of daily living, including bathing, dressing, eating, using the toilet, taking medication, shopping for groceries, and managing money. People who need long-term care typically have a disability or chronic health condition that requires them to get help with one or more of the activities of daily living. This care can be provided at home by family, friends, or home health aides, through community-based services, in an assisted living facility, or in a skilled nursing home.

In the very early stages of Alzheimer's, my mom didn't really need any help. Her memory loss wasn't affecting her ability to care for herself or stay on top of her finances. By the time it became quite obvious that she was having trouble remembering things, I had to take away the car keys and hire someone to drive her on errands. I started keeping closer tabs on her finances by monitoring her mail for sweepstakes entry forms and donation solicitations from groups to which she had no ties. And I monitored her bank account online.

Within a couple of years, as it became more difficult for her to prepare her own meals and take care of her house, I moved her in with me. I gave her the medication she was taking daily and took her to her doctor's appointments. I made sure she ate breakfast and provided her with dinner every night. And I hired a home health aide – who was paid by the hour – to help her during the day while I worked. If my family traveled, we took my mom with us or lined up full-time care for her.

But it became increasingly difficult to care for her in my home. I had three young children who needed my constant care and attention. But what they got was an exhausted, stressed-out mom who was stretched to the limit by juggling work, household duties, and caring for her mom. The bigger problem, though, was that I didn't think my mom was safe. I was afraid that she would wander off because she lived in a separate apartment in my house that had its own entrance. Of course, I couldn't lock the door to her apartment from the outside. So she could come and go, which meant she could decide to take a walk on her own and end up getting lost. Plus, the apartment was on the second floor – which meant there was a risk of her falling down the stairs.

I talked to her about living someplace where she could get round-the-clock care in a safe environment. But she would forget we had those conversations within five minutes. So I visited memory-care facilities (assisted living facilities that provide specialized care for people with dementia) and chose one for her. I hated that I had to make this decision for her and that we hadn't talked *before* she developed Alzheimer's disease about the possibility that she might need this sort of care. However, the good news is that moving her into an assisted living facility was actually much easier – and less emotional – than moving her out of her house and into my home (which I describe in the next chapter). She simply said, "So I'm living here now." I answered, "Yes," and she settled right in and started making friends.

My mom is a social person, so living in a place where she is surrounded with others actually is great for her. It's been six years since she moved into assisted living, and she still participates in daily activities with other residents to the extent that she can. When I'm with her, I can enjoy being her daughter rather than feel stressed about being in a role of caregiver. There are aides who help her bathe, dress, eat, and use the toilet. If you become a caregiver for your parent, these are all things you might have to do. (Yes, men, you might have to bathe your mom.)

This care has come with a high cost – more than $300,000 over six years. Her monthly Social Security benefit covers about half of the cost. Because my mom does not have long-term care insurance, I've used her retirement savings, proceeds from the sale of her house, and an inheritance from her parents to pay for the rest. It's taken some very careful planning to make sure the money she has lasts long enough to cover her care.

OPTIONS FOR CARE

If your parent needs care, there are several options. Under-standing and exploring these options before care is needed is important because it will help you and your parent figure out what is affordable and what will meet his or her needs over time. Keep in mind that care doesn't have to be provided in just one setting. Your parent might be able to receive care at home, then move to a facility as he or she needs a higher level of care.

When weighing options for care, it's also important to con-sider your family's values. Many cultures expect that the family will care for its elder members. That might mean that you need to take steps sooner rather than later to bolster your finances or make adjustments (such as moving to a house that can accom-modate your parent) so you can be a caregiver.

You might also want to consider hiring a geriatric care manager – also called an aging life care professional – who can help evaluate housing options for your parent, coordinate care, and assist with the financial issues, such as filing insurance claims. The biggest benefit of working with an aging life care professional is that you get a third party who can facilitate difficult conversations about long-term care with your parent. You can find one near you through the Aging Life Care Association's website at www.aginglifecare.org.

At home: As I mentioned, most people prefer to stay in their homes. It can work if there is someone – either a friend, family member, or professional – who can provide care and if the house meets your parent's needs. Professional in-home care services range from companion care providers who help people who need a low-level of assistance to personal care assistants who help with the activities of daily living such as dressing, bathing, and preparing meals, to nursing assistants who can provide some medical care. The median hourly cost of a home health aide is $22, according to Genworth's 2018 Cost of Care Survey. [12]

You can find in-home care services near you at Caring.com. You also can contact the local Area Agency on Aging to learn about home health agencies. To get the contact information for your local AAA, call the Eldercare Locator at 800-677-1116 or visit https://eldercare.acl.gov. If your parent lives in a rural area, there might not be any home care service agencies. In that case, you might need to reach out to your parents' friends, neighbors, or place of worship to get recommendations for caregivers in the area. If you will be your parent's caregiver and your parent can afford to pay for care, consider talking to your parent about getting paid for the services you provide – especially if you're giving up a full-time job to be a caregiver. If your parent agrees, work with an elder law attorney to draw up a contract that spells out your scope of work and the payment you'll receive.

Home care isn't always the best option, though, if the house isn't set up to accommodate a parent experiencing physical or cognitive decline. For example, Debra Newman,[13] founder and CEO of Newman Long Term Care, which is one of the largest long-term care insurance brokerage firms in the U.S., had clients who lived in a house with a spiral staircase. Each morning, the wife helped her husband get up and dressed then held his belt to prevent him from falling as he walked down the stairs. At night, he would hold onto her as she walked up the stairs. It wasn't a safe situation for either of them, and the couple really needed to be in assisted living, Newman said.

Adult day care: This community-based service is an affordable alternative to home health care. Linda Fodrini-Johnson,[14] founder of Eldercare Services and a care manager with more than 30 years of experience, said she often turns to adult day care when she has clients who can't afford to quit a job to care for a parent and the parent can't afford full-time home care. Adult day care services provide transportation, social activities, meals, and support services in stand-alone centers or in connection with senior centers, churches, or hospitals. You can find adult day care services by searching the National Adult Day Services Association's database at www.nadsa.org, by contacting your local Area Agency on Aging, by or contacting your state's adult day services association. The median monthly cost of adult day care services is $1,560, according to Genworth's Cost of Care Survey.

Assisted living: Assisted living facilities have staff who can provide round-the-clock help with the daily activities of living, such as bathing, dressing, and meal preparation. They do not provide skilled nursing care, but they might have a nurse on staff. Residents typically have the option of a private or semi-private room (a shared room, which will cost less). They tend to provide daily activities – and even outings – to keep residents engaged. Caring.com and APlaceforMom.com offer guides about choosing assisted living and searchable databases to find facilities. The median monthly cost of assisted living is $4,000, according to Genworth's Cost of Care Survey.

Memory care: There are assisted living facilities that provide specialized care for people with memory loss. Like traditional assisted living facilities, memory care facilities provide help with daily activities of living. However, they are secure facilities that are locked to prevent residents from wandering outside, and they provide specialized care tailored to the needs of people with dementia or other cognitive impairments. Sometimes assisted living facilities have memory care units within them. If your parent needs this sort of care, look for a facility that has nurses on staff or contracts with a medical care provider to come to the facility because makes it so much easier to get medical care for a parent with dementia. It allows your parent to be treated for minor issues in familiar surroundings rather than having to leave the facility to see a doctor, which can be incredibly confusing – even traumatic – for someone with dementia.

Genworth's Cost of Care Survey doesn't provide the median cost of memory care, but it tends to be higher than assisted living yet lower than skilled nursing.[15] You can find guides for choosing memory care facilities and search for facilities in your area at Caring.com and APlaceforMom.com.

Skilled nursing: These licensed health care facilities provide 24-hour medical care, which your parent might need in the late stages of Alzheimer's or if a medical condition has left your parent unable to function independently. The care in these facilities is typically provided by registered nurses, certified nurse assistants, and physical, speech and occupational therapists.[16] And it's a higher level of care than what is provided in assisted living facilities. Medicare.gov has a guide to choosing a nursing home and detailed information about every Medicare- and Medicaid-certified facility at www.medicare.gov/nursinghomecompare/search .html. As I said, Medicaid does cover nursing home care, but Medicare will cover only short stays after hospitalization. The median monthly cost of nursing home care is $7,441 in a semi-private room and $8,365 in a private room, according to Genworth's 2018 Cost of Care Survey.[17]

Masonic homes: The fraternal organization of Freemasons has senior living homes in communities across the U.S. that provide varying levels of care, including at-home care.[18] Many are open to the public, not just to Masons. Some offer care regardless of ability to pay if certain requirements are met.[19] And some offer a life care plan (typically for Masons) that allows residents to give a majority of their assets to the Masonic home in return for a lifetime of care, even if the assets don't cover the entire cost of care.[20] To find a Masonic home, search "masonic home" and the city or state where your parent lives.

WAYS TO PAY FOR LONG-TERM CARE AT HOME OR IN A FACILITY

Although long-term care can be expensive, there are ways to soften the blow. But that takes planning – which is why I'm advocating that you talk to your parents sooner rather than later to find out whether they have a plan and to formulate one if they don't. Here's what you need to know about the various ways to pay for long-term care.

Long-term care insurance: One of the first money conversations I had with my mom was about long-term care insurance. Well, before she was diagnosed with Alzheimer's, I suggested that she look into getting a policy. I simply said she should consider getting this type of insurance because it would help pay for care if she ever needed it. She took my advice and met with an insurance agent, but unfortunately was denied coverage because of another medical condition. If I had been smart, I would've used that opportunity to discuss her finances and create a plan of action in case she ever needed care – but I dropped that ball.

If my mom had been able to buy long-term care insurance, it would've paid for care in a nursing home, an assisted living facility, or in her home – which is where most people prefer to get care. There's a myth that long-term care insurance is unaffordable for most people, Newman said. To be clear, it's not cheap. But the younger you are when you get a policy, the more affordable it usually is. For example, Newman said a 55-year-old couple buying a policy together could get coverage for $125 a month each. "I would call that affordable," she said – especially when you consider that the median monthly cost of a home health aide is about $4,000 and skilled nursing care is more than $8,000. If your parents are in their 60s and still in good health, they can get a policy with a decent premium, Newman said. If they're already in their 70s or have health issues, keep reading for other options that might work better for them because they might not qualify for long-term care insurance.

When getting a long-term care insurance policy, there are four key things to consider:

- How much of a monthly benefit does your parent want in today's dollars? To figure out how much coverage is needed, Newman recommends researching how much home health care costs where you live. Because most people get long-term care in their homes, your parent will want a benefit that can cover the cost of this sort of care (or a large percentage of it). You can use Genworth's Cost of Care calculator at https://www.genworth.com/aging-and-you/finances/cost-of-care.html to find out the median costs of various types of care in your area.
- How long does your parent want the benefit to last? Policies with unlimited benefits used to be more common, but now more companies tend to issue policies with benefits limited to a certain number of years. Newman said the average long-term care insurance claim is three years. The maximum benefit will then be calculated based on the monthly benefit you want and the number of years you want the benefit to last. So a $5,000 monthly benefit with a four-year benefit period would provide a maximum

benefit of $240,000 that could be used to cover long-term care costs.

- How long of an elimination period does your parent want? The deductible for long-term care insurance is called the elimination or waiting period. It's the number of days the policy holder is willing to pay for long-term care costs out of pocket before insurance coverage kicks in. Elimination periods are usually 30, 60, or 90 days. Opting for a longer elimination period can help keep down the cost of insurance.
- Does your parent want inflation protection? Just like the cost of pretty much any other good or service, the cost of long-term care rises each year. That's why long-term care policies offer inflation protection so benefits keep pace with the rising cost of care. Inflation protection is important, but it also makes coverage more expensive. Most people opt for 3 percent inflation protection, but opting for 1 percent will cost 30 percent less, Newman said.

There are several other ways to save money on a long-term care insurance policy. For example, a shared care rider that connects the policies of a couple – including people who are domestic partners – reduces the costs. Instead of having, say, two separate four-year benefits, the couple would have eight years between them – which also is a plus in case one partner needs more care than the other. Insurers also offer discounts of 10 percent or more to people who are in great health.[21] And most states have some sort of tax incentive for people to own long-term care insurance, Newman said. Premiums also qualify as a medical expense that can be deducted on federal tax returns if they exceed a certain percentage of the taxpayer's adjusted gross income.[22]

And self-employed workers may be able to deduct the cost of long-term care insurance as an expense.

Some employers offer employees long-term care insurance. Otherwise, one of the best ways to find the right policy at the right price is to connect with an insurance broker, such as Newman, who works with several companies and can help compare plans for you. You can find a broker through the American Association for Long-Term Care website, www.aaltci.org, or by calling 818-597-3227.

Life insurance with a long-term care benefit: If your parent doesn't like the idea of getting a long-term care insurance policy that he or she might never use, there's another option: a hybrid life insurance policy. These policies include a long-term care benefit that can be accessed if long-term care is needed. If that benefit is never used, the policy will pay out on your parent's death. With a hybrid life insurance policy, there's an option to make a single, lump-sum premium payment or monthly premium payments. These policies tend to be more expensive than traditional long-term care insurance because they also provide a death benefit, Newman said. Also, the premiums aren't tax deductible. So if your parents don't need life insurance, they will be better off sticking with a traditional long-term care insurance policy.

Annuities: If your parent doesn't qualify for long-term care insurance because of age or health reasons, an annuity might be an option – that is, if your parent has a large stash of cash to invest in an annuity. A lump-sum payment is made in exchange for a guaranteed stream of income over a specified period of time. Or if your parent already has an annuity, it can be transferred to a long-term care annuity, Newman said.

With an annuity that has a long-term care benefit, the payout will be more than the amount invested. For example, if you have a $100,000 annuity, you might get $200,000 in long-term care coverage, Newman said. Your parent still can tap the annuity even if he or she doesn't need the money for long-term care.

Another type of annuity that offers long-term care benefits is a medically underwritten immediate annuity. A typical annuity would provide monthly payouts based on a person's life expectancy. Medically underwritten annuities are ideal for people with Alzheimer's or a similar disease because they take into account that the annuity owner will have a shorter lifespan and will pay out more each month, Newman said.

Medicaid: This government program actually is the top payer in the nation for long-term care services.[23] It pays for care in skilled nursing facilities and at home[24] – but it typically does not cover care in an assisted living facility. In some states, Medicaid will even pay for family caregivers.[25] However, to be eligible for Medicaid, your parent must have limited income and assets. The income amount varies from state to state,[26] but typically countable assets must be $2,000 or less for individuals or $3,000 or less for couples.[27] Countable assets do not include a primary residence (your parent's home), household belongings, one vehicle, life insurance up to a certain amount, funds for burial up to a certain amount, and assets in specific kinds of trusts. It is possible to spend down assets – or even transfer assets – to qualify for Medicaid. But to do that, it's best to work with an elder law attorney who specializes in helping people qualify for Medicaid. You can find one through the National Academy of Elder Law Attorneys' website, www.naela.org.

To find out whether your parent qualifies for Medicaid coverage for long-term care, contact the local community-based services office. That office will help with the Medicaid application and, if your parent wants in-home care, will do an evaluation to determine how many hours of care your parent qualifies for, Fodrini-Johnson said. "That's either going to open the door or shut the door right away," she said. Even if you think your parent's income is too high to qualify, apply anyway because he or she might get a portion of care costs covered by Medicaid, Fodrini-Johnson said.

Veterans Affairs benefits: If your parent has a service-related disability, he or she can get nursing home care through the Department of Veterans Affairs.[28] However, if your parent has a long-term care need that isn't service-related, he or she might qualify for the VA's aid and attendance program,[29] which provides an increased monthly pension to cover the cost of care at home for veterans and their spouses,[30] or for veteran-directed care,[31] which provides a flexible budget for home or community-based care. To find a VA benefit office near your parent, visit www.va.gov/find-locations/ or call 844-698-2311.

Reverse mortgage: Your parents might be able to tap the equity in their home with a reverse mortgage to pay for long-term care. Adults 62 and older who own their home outright or have paid off most of their mortgage can apply for a reverse mortgage (also known as a Home Equity Conversion Mortgage) to access the equity that has built up in their home.[32] The money from a reverse mortgage can be received as a lump sum, in monthly payments, or as a line of credit.[33] To be clear, a reverse mortgage is a loan that has to be paid back. It doesn't have to be paid back while the homeowner still is living in the home – only when the house is sold or the homeowner moves out or dies. However, the loan balance does rise over time because interest is added to the balance each month.[34] Borrowers don't have to pay back more than the home is worth.[35] But there might not be any equity left in the home by the time it's sold if the reverse loan balance is a much as the value of the house – which means there will be no profits from the home sale.

Also, be aware that there are several fees associated with reverse mortgages – an origination fee, mortgage insurance premiums, and closing costs. And a study by the Consumer Financial Protection Bureau found that reverse mortgages are complex products that are difficult to understand and deceptive marketing is common.[36] So your parents should consider this option carefully. Even better, they should discuss with a financial planner whether it would make financial sense for them to use a reverse mortgage to pay for long-term care.

Self-pay: The majority of people who need long-term care receive help from unpaid caregivers, according to the Bipartisan Policy Center.[37] That means friends and family are taking care of them. If your parents don't have long-term care insurance (or a hybrid life insurance policy) and don't qualify for government benefits, there's a good chance they will have to rely on you for care – that is, unless they have enough in savings or other financial resources.

You parents could very well have factored in the cost of long-term care into their retirement planning. If that is the case, you need to discuss with them what resources they have and how you can access those resources if you are their power of attorney and will have to oversee the payment of their care. Depending on what type of accounts your parents have, withdrawals from those accounts could be taxed differently. That's important to keep in mind because taxes will reduce the funds that are available to pay for your parents' care.

For example, withdrawals from retirement plans such as a 401(k), 403(b), IRA, and SEP IRA are subject to income tax. However, if funds are withdrawn before the account owner turns $59\frac{1}{2}$, there's an additional 10 percent early withdrawal penalty.[38] There's another catch to these retirement accounts. Account owners are required to take minimum distributions starting at age $70\frac{1}{2}$. If they don't, the amount not withdrawn is taxed at 50 percent.[39] So you don't want to tap one of these retirement accounts too soon to pay for care, nor do you want to wait until your parents are well into their 70s to use this source of funds because of the steep penalty for failing to take required minimum distributions. It would be a good idea for you and your parents to work with an accountant or financial planner to develop a plan for withdrawing funds to pay for your parents' care.

REACTIONS TO ANTICIPATE FROM YOUR PARENTS

As I said, talking about long-term care can be difficult. However, focusing on the financial side might actually make the conversation easier. That's why you might want to approach the topic by asking you parents whether they have long-term care insurance. You could say you read an article about it and were wondering whether they had it and whether you should get it (remember, asking your parents for advice is a good way to get them talking). Or you could tell a story about how expensive long-term care was for someone you know (you could use my mom's story) and ask whether they had a plan for how they would pay for care if they needed it.

Of course, there's a good chance your parents might be entirely open to a discussion because they don't want to be a burden on you and want to have a plan for care that doesn't entail relying on you. However, if your parents push back, here are some reactions to expect from them and ways you can respond that might help them recognize the importance of planning for long-term care.

> **Parent:** "It won't happen to me."
> **You:** "I hope you never do need long-term care. But, unfortunately, more than two-thirds of people 65 and older end up needing long-term care. So the odds aren't really in your favor. That's why I think it would be a good idea to at least talk about how to pay for care if you ever need it. Medicare and health insurance won't pay for long-term care, but long-term care insurance will. There are some other options, too." (Then you could share the information I've provided in this chapter. You also could share a story of someone you know – or even create a story – who wasn't prepared to deal with a long-term care need.)
> **Parent:** "I don't have to worry about long-term care because your mom/dad/my partner will take care of me."
> **You:** "I'm sure your wife/husband/partner will want to help you. But what's going to happen if both of you are in your 80s and you need care and your significant other can't physically care for you? What if both of you end up needing care?

Or what if your spouse/partner is no longer around to take care of you? I might not be able to help because I have a full-time job and kids to take care of. I think we need to come up with a plan to deal with these worst-case scenarios."

Parent: "Insurance will be too expensive, and I don't want to waste my money on something I might not use."

You: "Actually, did you know that you might be able to get a tax credit or deduction if you have long-term care insurance? And there are other ways to save money on long-term care insurance (mention shared benefit policies, longer elimination periods, getting coverage while younger and healthy). Or if you want to make sure you get your money's worth, there are life insurance policies that offer long-term care benefits. So that sort of insurance will pay out one way or another. Plus, the monthly cost of insurance is a whole lot cheaper than the monthly cost of long-term care."

Parent: "Whatever you do, don't ever put me in a nursing home."

You: "A nursing home isn't your only option if you need care. If you have long-term care insurance, it will pay for care at home. Even Medicaid pays for care at home. But there might come a point when remaining in your house is no longer the best option. You might not be able to get up and down the stairs. You might need medical care that Mom/Dad/your partner or we, your kids, just can't provide. Sure, none of us ever wants to have to live in a nursing home. But getting care from medical professionals might be the best option if you no longer can get dressed, bathe, or go to the bathroom by yourself. However, if we start planning now, we can figure out how to keep you in your home as long as possible if you ever do need care."

As you have these conversations, remember to be respectful of your parents and understanding as they work through any fears they might have about long-term care. After all, you might need long-term care someday, too. So think about how you would want your loved ones to discuss this touchy topic with you.

NOTES

1. Nationwide Retirement Institute (2018), "Long-Term Care: Insights From the 2018 Nationwide Health Care and Long-Term Care Consumer Survey," https://nationwidefinancial.com/media/pdf/NFM-17455AO.pdf?_ga=2.191349034.1266470792.1545401316-1440804513.1545401316 (Accessed Jan. 3, 2019).
2. Bipartisan Policy Center (2017), "Financial Long-Term Services and Supports: Seeking Bipartisan Solutions in Politically Challenging Times," https://bipartisanpolicy.org/wp-content/uploads/2017/07/BPC-Health-Financing-Long-Term-Services-and-Supports.pdf (Accessed Jan. 3, 2019).
3. Bipartisan Policy Center (2017), "Financial Long-Term Services and Supports: Seeking Bipartisan Solutions in Politically Challenging Times," https://bipartisanpolicy.org/wp-content/uploads/2017/07/BPC-Health-Financing-Long-Term-Services-and-Supports.pdf (Accessed Jan. 3, 2019).
4. Bipartisan Policy Center (2017), "Financial Long-Term Services and Supports: Seeking Bipartisan Solutions in Politically Challenging Times," https://bipartisanpolicy.org/wp-content/uploads/2017/07/BPC-Health-Financing-Long-Term-Services-and-Supports.pdf (Accessed Jan. 3, 2019).
5. Bipartisan Policy Center (2017), "Financial Long-Term Services and Supports: Seeking Bipartisan Solutions in Politically Challenging Times," https://bipartisanpolicy.org/wp-content/uploads/2017/07/BPC-Health-Financing-Long-Term-Services-and-Supports.pdf (Accessed Jan. 3, 2019).
6. LongTermCare.gov, "What Is Medicare and What Does It Cover?" https://longtermcare.acl.gov/medicare-medicaid-more/medicare.html (Accessed Jan. 3, 2019).
7. Genworth, (2018), "Cost of Care Survey 2019," https://www.genworth.com/aging-and-you/finances/cost-of-care.html (Accessed Jan. 3, 2019).
8. LongTermCare.gov, "What Is Covered by Health & Disability Insurance," https://longtermcare.acl.gov/costs-how-to-pay/what-is-covered-by-health-disability-insurance/index.html (Accessed Jan. 3, 2019).
9. Bipartisan Policy Center (2017), "Financial Long-Term Services and Supports: Seeking Bipartisan Solutions in Politically Challenging Times," https://bipartisanpolicy.org/wp-content/uploads/2017/07/BPC-Health-Financing-Long-Term-Services-and-Supports.pdf (Accessed Jan. 3, 2019).

10. Associated Press-NORC Center for Public Affairs Research, "Long-Term Caregiving: The True Costs of Caring for Aging Adults," https://www .longtermcarepoll.org/project/long-term-caregiving-the-true-costs-of-caring-for-aging-adults/ (Accessed Jan. 3, 2019).

11. LongTermCare.gov, "What Is Long-Term Care?" https://longter mcare.acl.gov/the-basics/what-is-long-term-care.html (Accessed Jan. 3, 2019).

12. Genworth (2018), "Cost of Care Survey 2019," https://www.genworth .com/aging-and-you/finances/cost-of-care.html (Accessed Jan. 3, 2019).

13. Debra Newman, https://www.linkedin.com/in/debracnewman/ (Accessed Jan. 3, 2019).

14. Linda Fodrini-Johnson, https://www.linkedin.com/in/lindafodrini johnson/ (Accessed Jan. 3, 2019).

15. Caring.com, "What Is Memory Care?" https://www.caring.com/senior-living/memory-care-facilities (Accessed Jan. 3, 2019).

16. Aging Care, Marlo Sollitto, "What's the Difference Between Skilled Nursing and a Nursing Home?" https://www.agingcare.com/articles /difference-skilled-nursing-and-nursing-home-153035.htm (Accessed Jan. 3, 2019).

17. Genworth (2018), "Cost of Care Survey 2019," https://www.genworth .com/aging-and-you/finances/cost-of-care.html (Accessed Jan. 3, 2019).

18. SeniorLiving.org, "Masonic Senior Care Organizations," https:// www.seniorliving.org/basics/special-interest-groups/masonic-senior-housing/ (Accessed Jan. 3, 2019).

19. Masonic Communities of Kentucky, "About Masonic Communities," http://www.masonichomesky.com/about-us/ (Accessed Jan. 3, 2019).

20. Masonic Home of Florida, http://www.masonichomefl.com/admissions .html (Accessed Jan. 3, 2019).

21. Life Happens, "What You Need to Know About Long-Term Care Insurance," file:///C:/Users/Alex/Downloads/LifeHappens%20Guide%202 018%20Branded.pdf (Accessed Jan. 3, 2019).

22. Newman Long Term Care, "IRS Issues Long-Term Care Premium Deductibility Limits for 2018," https://www.newmanlongtermcare.com /2016/11/irs-issues-long-term-care-premium-deductibility-limits-for-2018/.

23. Medicaid.gov, (2016) "Long Term Services & Supports," https://www .medicaid.gov/medicaid/ltss/index.html (Accessed Jan. 3, 2019).

24. LongTermCare.gov, "State Medicaid Programs," https://longtermcare .acl.gov/medicare-medicaid-more/medicaid/index.html (Accessed Jan. 3, 2019).

25. Kristen Hicks (2018), "How to Become a Paid Family Caregiver," A Place for Mom, https://www.aplaceformom.com/blog/how-to-become-a-paid-family-caregiver/ (Accessed Jan. 3, 2019).

26. LongTermCare.gov, "Financial Requirements," https://longtermcare .acl.gov/medicare-medicaid-more/medicaid/medicaid-eligibility/finan cial-requirements.html (Accessed Jan. 3, 2019).

27. LongTermCare.gov, "Financial Requirements: Assets," https://longterm care.acl.gov/medicare-medicaid-more/medicaid/medicaid-eligibility /financial-requirements-assets.html (Accessed Jan. 3, 2019).

28. U.S. Department of Veterans Affairs, "VA Nursing Homes, Assisted Living, and Home Health Care," https://www.va.gov/health-care/about-va-health-benefits/long-term-care/ (Accessed Jan. 3, 2019).

29. U.S. Department of Veterans Affairs, "Aid & Attendance and Housebound," https://www.benefits.va.gov/pension/aid_attendance_house bound.asp (Accessed Jan. 3, 2019).

30. LongTermCare.gov, "Veterans Affairs Benefits," https://longtermcare .acl.gov/medicare-medicaid-more/veterans-affairs-benefits.html (Accessed Jan. 3, 2019).

31. U.S. Department of Veterans Affairs, "Veteran-Directed Care," https:// www.va.gov/geriatrics/guide/longtermcare/veteran-directed_care.asp (Accessed Jan. 3, 2019).

32. U.S. Department of Housing and Urban Development, "How the HECM Program Works," https://www.hud.gov/program_offices/housing/sfh/ hecm/hecmabou (Accessed Jan. 3, 2019).

33. LongTermCare.gov, "Reverse Mortgages," https://longtermcare.acl.gov /costs-how-to-pay/paying-privately/reverse-mortages/index.html (Accessed Jan. 3, 2019).

34. Consumer Financial Protection Bureau (2018), "Considering a Reverse Mortgage?" https://pueblo.gpo.gov/Publications/pdfs/6107 .pdf (Accessed Jan. 3, 2019).

35. Consumer Financial Protection Bureau (2018) "Reverse Mortgages: A Discussion Guide," https://pueblo.gpo.gov/Publications/pdfs/6271.pdf (Accessed Jan. 3, 2019).

36. Megan Thibos, (2012) "Understanding Reverse Mortgages," Consumer Financial Protection Bureau, https://www.consumerfinance.gov/about-us/blog/understanding-reverse-mortgages/ (Accessed Jan. 3, 2019).

37. Bipartisan Policy Center (2017), "Financial Long-Term Services and Supports: Seeking Bipartisan Solutions in Politically Challenging Times," https://bipartisanpolicy.org/wp-content/uploads/2017/07/BPC-Health-Financing-Long-Term-Services-and-Supports.pdf (Accessed Jan. 3, 2019).

38. IRS (2018), "Retirement Topics: Exceptions to Tax on Early Distributions," https://www.irs.gov/retirement-plans/plan-participant-employee/retirement-topics-tax-on-early-distributions (Accessed Jan. 3, 2019).

39. IRS (2018), "Retirement Plan and IRA Required Minimum Distribution FAQs," https://www.irs.gov/retirement-plans/retirement-plans-faqs-regarding-required-minimum-distributions (Accessed Jan. 3, 2019).

13

Talking to Your Parents About When It's Time to Move

My mom loved working in her garden. When she moved into her own house after divorcing my father, her backyard was basically a blank slate. There was a concrete patio and little else. Over the years, she turned it into a lush landscape with flowers, fruit trees, herbs, vegetables, and even a grape arbor. When the weather was warm, if she wasn't working in her garden she was enjoying spending time there with friends and family.

But it became harder for her to maintain her yard after she developed Alzheimer's disease in her 60s. Operating the lawn mower became a struggle for my mom, so my husband started mowing the grass for her. She let the bushes and flower beds become overgrown. She stopped planting vegetables and herbs. The more her memory declined, the more her garden did, too.

It wasn't just her yard that my mom could no longer care for. Her three-bedroom house also became too much of an undertaking for her. She didn't let it become dirty, but she didn't clean it as well. Clutter started accumulating. Repairs needed to be made but weren't.

There was a bigger problem, though. I had hired someone to take her on errands and keep her company during the day. But the aide wasn't there all day or at night – which meant my mom was alone and at risk a lot of the time.

I knew my mom loved her house, but I also knew that she could no longer live there. She wasn't safe alone. And we couldn't afford to hire full-time care then knowing that she likely would need to use what financial resources she had to pay for assisted living down the road. So I told her I thought it would be best for her to move in with me.

It was a conversation I never wanted to have, but it was necessary. It might be necessary for you, too, to have this discussion with your parents now or at some point as they age.

What makes this conversation so hard is the fact that most older adults don't want to move from the homes they've lived in for years – even when deep down they know they should. A 2018 AARP survey found that 76 percent of Americans 50 and older want to stay in their current home as they age.[1] However, just 46 percent expect they'll be able to stay in their current home.

Of course, there's no need to push your parents to move if they're in good health, they can afford to maintain their home, and it continues to meet their needs as they age. But there certainly are situations like my mom's when moving makes sense – and your parents might need encouragement (not nagging) from you to make this choice. Here are some key signs that you need to talk to your Mom or Dad about moving.

Your parent has memory issues. Pay attention to signs that your parent is having memory problems. You might notice that your parent's once-clean and organized home is now cluttered, the refrigerator is filled with expired or many duplicate items, and there are reminders posted around the house. If Mom or Dad can't remember what year or month it is or forgets conversations shortly after having them, don't write it off as a part of old age. Your parent needs to visit a doctor to be screened for dementia.

If your parent has dementia and is alone, it's time to start talking about a safer living arrangement. He could wander off, fall while going to the bathroom at night, become a victim of scammers, or set the house on fire while trying to make a meal (that's no joke – my mom almost did). Family members or hired aides could help your parent stay in his home. But there could come a point when he needs to move in with family, an assisted living facility, or a nursing home.

Your parent has health issues. It might be time for your parent or parents to move if they have health issues that are making it difficult for them to maintain their house on their own. Health issues might also be making it unsafe for them to live in their house if they're having trouble getting up and down the stairs or into the bathtub.

Your parent's house is a financial burden. High housing costs force about one-third of adults 50 and older to pay more than 30 percent of their income for homes, forcing them to cut back on essentials and retirement savings, according to a report by the Harvard Joint Center for Housing Studies and AARP Foundation.[2] And homeowners with mortgages are more likely to work longer and retire at a later age than those whose mortgages are paid off, according to Boston College's Center for Retirement Research.[3] In short, your parents' home could be hurting their ability to retire.

It could make financial sense for them to downsize sooner rather than later to increase their chances of retiring when they want. If they're already retired and repairs, utility bills, property taxes, and mortgage payments are draining their savings faster than they'd like, it might be time for you to let them know it's okay to let go of the family home so they have enough money for a comfortable retirement.

Your parent is isolated. An AARP survey found that 30 percent of older adults said they lack companionship, feel left out, or feel isolated from others.[4] If your parent is among them, that can be a problem. Loneliness has been linked to a whole host of problems – from health risks to cognitive decline to higher mortality rates, according to a National Institutes of Health report.[5] If Mom or Dad lives alone and doesn't have a network of friends or family nearby, moving to retirement community with others his or her age could make sense.

If any of these situations apply to your parents, consider talking to them about moving. Of course, it's ultimately their decision (except in extreme cases where they're no longer mentally capable of making that sort of decision). But to increase your chances of having a productive conversation and persuading your parents to move, you need to communicate carefully.

HIGHLIGHT THE POSITIVE

Because your parents could be very attached to their home and their community, the idea of moving might seem painful to them. I know my mom didn't want to have to give up her house and her garden – even though she probably realized it was becoming too difficult for her to stay where she was. That's why I focused on the positive aspects of moving rather than the reasons why she couldn't stay in her house.

Fortunately, the house I lived in had two apartments in it. I told my mom that by moving in with me, she still could have her own space. She could decorate it as she wanted. She could put potted plants on the balcony and sit outside whenever the weather was nice. She could help me in my small yard. Because I lived a block from the downtown square, she could walk to restaurants, art galleries, and concerts in the park (with me or her aide, of course). I told her that I could help make meals for her, or she could eat with my family. I told her she would be able to spend more time with her grandkids. And I told her I would be right there if she needed help with anything.

Highlighting all of the positive aspects of moving into my home helped me persuade my mom to sell her house. It still was difficult for her to say goodbye to her home. And I hated having to be the one to talk her into leaving it. But it was a necessary conversation that led to a much safer housing situation for my mom. Unfortunately, my mom had to move again into assisted living once it became clear that she needed a higher level of care (which I discussed in Chapter 12).

You, too, will need to highlight the positive aspects of moving if you want to increase the chances that your parents will listen to your advice. Avoid saying anything negative like, "You can't stay where you are." They'll feel like you're trying to take away their independence and might dig their heels in about staying in their house.

FOCUS ON THE FINANCIAL BENEFITS OF MOVING

Even if money is a taboo topic in your family, you might have luck getting through to your parents if you talk about all the ways that moving can save them money. After all, most people are looking for ways to cut costs. By pointing out how they can reduce their biggest cost – housing – you could make some headway. But don't make it all about the math, cautions Mike McGrath,[6] a financial planner who persuaded his own parents to move. Paint a picture for them of how reducing housing costs will free up more money for things they enjoy or are important to them. That's what McGrath, who is senior vice president of EP Wealth Advisors, did when he could see that the 2,400-square-foot home his parents had lived in for 52 years was no longer working for them.

Both of his parents had health problems that were making it hard for them to get up and down the stairs. On top of that, they couldn't keep up with the maintenance physically. "They were always having people coming over to fix things," McGrath said. They also were saddled with a home equity loan and credit card debt they had taken on to help pay for McGrath and his sister to go to college. "They felt this weight on them," McGrath said.

So when his parents would make comments about the problems they were having with the house, McGrath would use those opportunities to mention the idea of moving. He helped them search online for one-story houses, making it feel like it was their idea to move. Once they got comfortable talking with him about their debt, he started showing them how they could pay it off if they sold their house. "It kind of opened their eyes," he said. Then he tapped into their emotions by pointing out how freeing it would be if they could wipe out their debt.

However, it still took a while before they came to grips with the fact that they'd be better off moving. "They finally surrendered to it," McGrath said. "The emotion of feeling they could be freer financially and emotionally was better than the emotion of hanging onto a house that was too big for them and falling apart."

His parents sold their house in March 2018 and rented an apartment with half the square footage of their house. They were able to pay off all of their debts by selling their home – which eliminated the $1,500 monthly debt payments they were making. And their rent is a couple hundred dollars less than their mortgage, McGrath said. Selling their home also gave his parents a big stash of cash they could use for emergencies and for fun – such as buying Christmas gifts for the grandkids, which McGrath said his mom loves to do.

They're much more at peace now that they're not financially burdened by their house. "That's how you have to position it," he said. You have to help your parents understand how much easier things could be for them financially if they moved.

FOCUS ON THE SOCIAL BENEFITS OF MOVING

Maybe you've noticed that your Mom is lonely now that Dad is gone. Or Dad doesn't get out as much anymore because he doesn't like driving in traffic or using public transportation. It could be that both of your parents still are living in the large home where you grew up and the neighbors are now all young families. Whatever the reason might be, you think that your parent or parents would be better off moving to a place with more people their age. But in their minds, they think you want to ship them off to an old folks' home where they'll sit around and play Bingo all day. I don't blame them for balking because that seems depressing. But if you choose your words carefully and frame it right, you might be able to sell your parents on the idea of moving to a place geared to their age group.

Retirement communities actually are a lot hipper and fun these days. Heck, you can even be wastin' away again in Latitude Margaritaville, a retirement community inspired by the music of Jimmy Buffett with locations in Florida and South Carolina.[7] In fact, there are lots of so-called active adult communities that cater to a variety of interests[8] and offer amenities[9] ranging from golf to water activities to social events. Let your parents know there are plenty of places they might love to call home because they'll be surrounded by people their age and will have ample opportunities to be social.

Of course, there are other options beyond retirement communities that will allow your parents to remain social as they age. Relocating from the country to the city could give them access to public transportation and more entertainment options. Moving from a house to an apartment or condominium could give them an opportunity to interact with others more often. Or you might suggest that they move closer to you or other family members (that is, if you don't mind hanging out with your parents). Even assisted living facilities can help older adults facing physical or mental decline avoid becoming isolated. At both of the memory care facilities where my mom has lived, they have kept residents engaged throughout the day with activities, exercise, and group dining. The point you want to make is that your parents might actually be able to enjoy life more if they move to the right place.

FOCUS ON THE LONG-TERM BENEFITS

As I wrote in Chapter 12, there's a good chance at least one of your parents – perhaps even both – will need long-term care. I can tell you from experience that it's so much better to get them thinking about this possibility and planning for it rather than scrambling to deal with it once there's already a need. When my mom needed to move into an assisted living facility, I had to choose one for her. I feel like I made the right choice. But it would've been much easier if I had discussed with her before she developed dementia what sort of place she would want to live in if she needed long-term care.

If your parents can afford it, there are continuing care retirement communities that allow older adults to age in place – from independent living to assisted living and skilled nursing care options. CCRCs typically require that you be able to live independently when you move in, according to senior living referral service A Place for Mom.[10] And you have to pay an entry fee that can range from $100,000 to $1 million.[11]

But if you end up needing assisted living or nursing home care, that's part of the package with CCRCs – which can eliminate a lot of the stress that comes with trying to figure out long-term care. Letting your parents know that such options exist might get them thinking about the benefits of moving. They might realize that living in a CCRC – or even picking out assisted living facilities that they'd be willing to move to if the need arises – would lift a burden off you.

BE PATIENT AND COMPASSIONATE

You might recognize that it's time for your parents to move, but they might not want to leave a home they've been in for decades. That's why you have to be patient and give them time to accept that they could be better off by moving.

Although McGrath knew it was time for his parents to move to be in a better situation physically and to free some pressure financially, he didn't want to push too hard because he knew they were attached to their house. "Those things had to get to the point where they were more important than their house," he said. That actually took a few years from the time McGrath started encouraging his parents to move to when they actually did.

Even though they sold their home and moved into an apartment, McGrath is hoping his parents will take him up on his offer to move in with his family. His mom was flattered that he wanted them to live with him, but McGrath's dad politely declined. Still, McGrath is adding on a unit to his house that either his parents or his wife's parents could live in. He's hoping that when his parents' apartment lease comes up for renewal, they might be ready to move into his house. But he's not forcing them to make a decision. Instead, he said he's let them know, "If it ever becomes a good fit for you, that would be great."

When my friend Elizabeth's father died, she thought her mom would be better off living in a retirement community so she could be around other people her age and wouldn't have to worry about maintaining her house. But Elizabeth admits that she didn't do a good job of explaining the benefits of residences geared toward retirees (remember, it's important to use the right wording). "She said, "I'm not in the grave yet.' In her mind she thought I was trying to put her in a nursing home and assisted living," Elizabeth said about her mom's reluctance to move. "I pushed as much as I could, but she resisted. I didn't do a good enough job. I tried to explain it to her. I didn't say 'independent' enough. She just wouldn't listen. She tuned it out."

It didn't help that one of Elizabeth's brothers was telling her mother not to sell the house she'd lived in for 58 years because he had an emotional attachment to it. And her other brother was trying to talk her into moving closer to him. Neither wanted her to move into a retirement community. As I wrote in Chapter 5, the three siblings hadn't agreed about what would be best for their mom before talking to her about her living arrangements after her husband – their dad – had died. So Elizabeth's mom ended up buying a house in the city where her brothers live.

"Now she's in her house, and she's miserable because she's lonely," Elizabeth said. Plus, she's seeing the upkeep of the house is hard. Her sons haven't been able to help her, and she can't afford to hire someone to do the work. In fact, Elizabeth's mom realized less than two years after moving that buying a home was a mistake – and she admitted that to Elizabeth.

"She said, 'I see now why you were pushing the retirement community,'" Elizabeth said. "I pushed initially but backed off. But now my mom is coming to me." However, Elizabeth has told her mom that they shouldn't rush to move her again. "I told her we got caught off guard because we were in a rush. 'We're not going to do that this time,'" she told her mom. "'Let's take the next couple of years to explore it to find what's best for you.'"

HELP YOUR PARENTS EXPLORE HOUSING OPTIONS

Your parents might initially resist your attempts to even get them to consider moving. But that doesn't mean they'll never change their minds – as you can see from both Mike McGrath's and my friend Elizabeth's experiences. It just takes patience, perseverance, and, above all, compassion on your part. After all, what you might see as a house that's a financial drain on your parents, your parents see as a home that's full of memories. So give them time. Encourage your parents to share what they enjoy about their home but help them come to terms with the drawbacks of remaining where they are. Giving them that opportunity to talk about the pros and cons – while you listen – might help them realize sooner rather than later that it's time to move.

As they become more open to the idea of moving, you can help them explore their options. With so many types of housing now available, they're likely to find something that suits their needs and is in their price range.

- **Active Adult Communities:** These communities offer independent living in low-maintenance homes for adults 55 and older, have a whole host of resort-like amenities, and tend to be located near health care facilities, shopping, and entertainment options. You can help your parents search for active adult communities at 55Places .com, which also provides an annual list of the 55 best active adult communities.[12] Costs can vary widely.[13]

- **Independent Living Communities:** Like active adult communities, these communities tend to be age-restricted. Housing options can include apartments, condominiums, or houses. Some may include housekeeping services, meals, and social programs.[14] Costs can range from $1,500 to $10,000 a month, according to Senior Living.org.[15] You can search for independent living options at APlaceforMom.com and SeniorLiving.org.

- **HUD-Sponsored Senior Housing:** Affordable housing options are available to low-income seniors through U.S. Department of Housing and Urban Development programs – including public housing, multifamily subsidized housing and housing vouchers for privately owned rentals. You can get more information at https://www .hud.gov/topics/information_for_senior_citizens.

- **Continuing Care Retirement Communities**: These communities offer independent living, assisted living, and nursing home care on one campus so adults can age in place. These communities tend to be the most expensive housing option, with entrance fees ranging from $100,000 to $1 million and monthly fees ranging from $3,000 to $5,000, according to AARP.[16] You can search for CCRCs at RetirementLiving.com.

- **Residential Care Homes**: These facilities offer housing and care (such as meals and assistance with activities of daily living) in a homelike setting for a small group of seniors. They can be cheaper than assisted living facilities, according to A Place for Mom.[17] You can search for residential care homes at APlaceforMom.com and SeniorLiving.com.

- **Assisted Living:** If your parents need help with bathing, dressing, walking, or other daily living activities, an assisted living facility might be ideal for them. They typically can choose from studio, one-bedroom, or two-bedroom units in the facilities. According to insurance company Genworth's Cost of Care Survey 2018, the median monthly cost for an assisted living facility is $4,000.[18] You can find assisted living facilities at APlaceforMom.com and SeniorLiving.org. The National Center for Assisted Living provides tips for choosing a facility at www.ahcancal.org/ncal.

- **Memory Care:** If your parents have dementia, they can get an additional level of care in a private or semi-private room in a memory care facility. These facilities are secure to prevent patients from wandering out of the building. Costs range from $3,000 to $6,000, according to SeniorLiving.org[19] –visit this site to search for memory care facilities.

- **Nursing Home:** Skilled nursing facilities provide 24-hour medical assistance for patients who are recovering from an injury, stroke, or other health issue or long-term care for patients who can no longer care for themselves. The median monthly cost is $7,441 for a semi-private room and $8,365 for a private room, according to Genworth's Cost of Care Survey 2018.[20] Medicare.gov has a "Nursing Home Compare" tool that provides detailed information about Medicare- and Medicaid-certified facilities at https://www.medicare.gov/nursinghomecompare/

search.html. You also can search for nursing homes on websites such as APlaceforMom.com and SeniorLiving .com.

NOTES

1. Joanne Binette and Kerri Vasold (2018), AARP, "2018 Home and Community Preferences: A National Survey of Adults Age 18-Plus," https://www.aarp.org/research/topics/community/info-2018/2018-home-community-preference.html (Accessed Jan. 3, 2019).

2. Harvard Joint Center for Housing Studies and AARP Foundation (2014), "U.S. Unprepared to Meet Housing Needs of Its Aging Population," http://www.jchs.harvard.edu/sites/jchs.harvard.edu/files/jchs_housing _americas_older_adults_2014_press_release_090214.pdf (Accessed Jan. 3, 2019).

3. Center for Retirement Research at Boston College (2014), "Retirement Delayed to Pay the Mortgage," http://squaredawayblog.bc.edu/squared-away/retirement-delayed-to-pay-the-mortgage-2/ (Accessed Jan. 3, 2019).

4. Joanne Binette and Kerri Vasold (2018), AARP, "2018 Home and Community Preferences: A National Survey of Adults Age 18-Plus," https://www.aarp.org/research/topics/community/info-2018/2018-home-community-preference.html (Accessed Jan. 3, 2019).

5. Erin York Cornwell and Linda J. Waite (2009), National Institutes of Health, "Social Disconnectedness, Perceived Isolation, and Health Among Older Adults," https://www.ncbi.nlm.nih.gov/pmc/articles/PMC2756979/ (Accessed Jan. 3, 2019).

6. Mike McGrath, https://www.epwealth.com/our-team/valencia/michael-mcgrath-cfp-clu/ (Accessed Jan. 3, 2019).

7. Latitude Margaritaville, https://www.latitudemargaritaville.com/ (Accessed Jan. 3, 2019).

8. SeniorLiving.org, "10 Unique Retirement Communities for Baby Boomers," https://www.seniorliving.org/retirement/unique-retirement-community/ (Accessed Jan. 3, 2019).

9. Investopedia, J.B. Maverick (2016), "Top 10 Active Retirement Communities in U.S.," https://www.investopedia.com/articles/retirement/082316/top-10-active-retirement-communities-us.asp (Accessed Jan. 3, 2019).

10. Jeff Anderson (2018), A Place for Mom, "What Are Continuing Care Retirement Communities (CCRCs)?" https://www.aplaceformom.com/blog/continuing-care-retirement-communities/ (Accessed Jan. 3, 2019).

11. AARP, "About Continuing Care Retirement Communities," https://www.aarp.org/caregiving/basics/info-2017/continuing-care-retirement-communities.html (Accessed Jan. 3, 2019).

12. Sean Keeley (2018), 55Places.com, "The 55 Best 55+ Active Adult Communities of 2018," https://www.55places.com/blog/the-55-best-55-active-adult-communities-of-2018 (Accessed Jan. 3, 2019).

13. SeniorLiving.org, "Senior Retirement Lifestyles," https://www.seniorliving.org/retirement/senior-lifestyles/ (Accessed Jan. 3, 2019).

14. A Place for Mom, "What Is Independent Living?" https://www.aplaceformom.com/independent-living (Accessed Jan. 3, 2019).

15. SeniorLiving.org, "Senior Retirement Lifestyles," https://www.seniorliving.org/retirement/senior-lifestyles/ (Accessed Jan. 3, 2019).

16. AARP, "About Continuing Care Retirement Communities," https://www.aarp.org/caregiving/basics/info-2017/continuing-care-retirement-communities.html (Accessed Jan. 3, 2019).

17. A Place for Mom, "What Is a Residential Care Home?" https://www.aplaceformom.com/care-homes (Accessed Jan. 3, 2019).

18. Genworth (2018), "Cost of Care Survey 2018," https://www.genworth.com/aging-and-you/finances/cost-of-care.html (Accessed Jan. 3, 2019).

19. SeniorLiving.org, "Finding the Best Memory Care Facility," https://www.seniorliving.org/lifestyles/memory-care/ (Accessed Jan. 3, 2019).

20. Genworth (2018), "Cost of Care Survey 2018," https://www.genworth.com/aging-and-you/finances/cost-of-care.html (Accessed Jan. 3, 2019).

14

If at First You Don't Succeed ...

Getting your parents to become comfortable with the idea of discussing their finances with you can take time. So if you've tried once or twice without luck, don't throw in the towel just yet. This is going to take some persistence.

I'm not suggesting that you act like a toddler in the checkout lane at the supermarket who won't stop badgering until he gets the candy he wants. You don't want to nag your parents to the point that they start avoiding you. But you shouldn't assume that because they've avoided money talks so far that you'll never get through to them.

"Trying to have conversations can't be a bad thing," said financial planner Daniel Lash.[1] "If you try many times and your parents aren't open, there's not much you can do. But if you tell them why it's important to you, most parents will talk. They will give you some feedback. They're not going to ignore you completely."

That's coming from someone who has talked to his own parents about their finances and has helped clients open the lines of communication with their parents. So with that in mind, here are some strategies that might help you get through to even the most reluctant parents.

GET A THIRD PARTY INVOLVED

Let's face it: Your parents might still think of you as a kid. You could be a 45-year-old doctor with a thriving practice, but your parents see you as that defiant teenager you once were. So it's no wonder they're having a hard time sharing financial details that they think are none of your business.

In that situation, getting a third party involved can help. Although your parents have resisted your efforts to get them to discuss their finances, they could be willing to open up to a financial planner, an attorney, a clergy member, or even a trusted friend, said eldercare expert Linda Fodrini-Johnson.[2]

You could reach out to any of those third parties your parents have a relationship with and ask that they encourage your parents to clue you in on key aspects of their finances. For example, you might know that your mom's sister has had conversations with her kids about her finances. So you could ask her to share with your mom how she and her children have benefitted from talking about what legal documents she has and what they need to know about her finances in case of an emergency.

If you reach out to an attorney or financial professionals your parents work with, be aware that they won't be able to share your parents' financial or legal information with you directly. But, hopefully, they will be willing to persuade your parents to talk to you. Or you could invite your parents to meet with your own financial planner, accountant, or attorney under the guise of wanting to share your information with them so they would know what to do if something happened to you. If you don't already work with a financial professional, you can find one through the following online resources:

- The Financial Planning Association's member directory at PlannerSearch.org
- The National Association of Personal Financial Advisors' directory at NAPFA.org
- The American Institute of CPAs' database of members at AICPA.org/forthepublic/findacpa.html
- The National Association of Estate Planners and Councils' database of Accredited Estate Planners at NAEPC.org

Another option is for you meet with an eldercare manager, also known as an aging life care manager or geriatric care manager. These professionals are experts in helping families communicate, solve problems, and plan for financial issues related to aging. You could describe your parents' personalities to the care manager to get an individualized approach for talking to them, Fodrini-Johnson said. The Aging Life Care Association has a member directory you can search on its website (AgingLifeCare.org) to find a professional near you.

USE MOTIVIATIONAL INTERVIEWING

Motivational what? Don't let the terminology scare you. Motivational interviewing is a counseling style that aims to help people who are resistant to change overcome their roadblocks to change. Financial psychologist Dr. Brad Klontz[3] said it's typically used for treating drug and alcohol addiction, but he recommends trying it if your parents are reluctant to share any information with you about their finances

Despite the name, the key to motivational interviewing is listening – listening to your parents' reasons why they don't want to have a conversation about their finances. Then, rather than ask them why they don't want to share information with you, reframe their statement. Here's an example of how it works.

Say you've tried to discuss the importance of having a will with your mom but she's always resisted your attempts to have a conversation – likely because talking about wills and estate planning forces her to think about death. So you try to bring up the topic once again.

> **You:** "Hey, Mom I think it's important that you get a will."
> **Mom:** "I don't need a will."
> **You:** "Okay. So you don't see any value in getting a will."
> **Mom:** "I'm not saying there's no value."
> **You:** "So you do think there is value in getting a will. Maybe we can talk about what the value would be for you."

If Mom continues to push back, Klontz said you could say something like, "So you feel it's not important for us to know what you want?"

Notice that this sample dialogue doesn't use the word "why." If you respond by asking "why," your parents could become defensive and take the opposite side of what you're hoping for, Klontz said. Motivational interviewing gets them to think about the reasons why they don't want to do or discuss what you're suggesting without confrontation and hopefully gets them to stop resisting you.

REMIND YOUR PARENTS ABOUT THEIR PARENTS

It might be time to pull out the big guns if your parents aren't budging. By that, I mean telling your parents not to make the mistakes their own parents made. Of course, you don't want to say something like, "You always complain about how you had to deal with the mess your dad created because he didn't have a will, but now you're going to do the same thing to me." But you can gently remind your parents of the struggles they encountered – or are still coping with – as a result of their parents' lack of financial planning or unwillingness to talk about money matters.

I used this tactic with my mom when I had to get her to surrender her car keys – which is arguably more difficult than getting parents to discuss their personal finances. When my mom was in the early stage of Alzheimer's disease, she started getting confused while driving and having trouble getting where she wanted to go. I knew I had to take away her keys to protect her and other people on the road. So I reminded her of what happened once with her father.

My mother had taken me and my younger sister to her parents' house and left us with her father while she went to check on her mother, who was in the hospital recovering from a heart attack. She made it very clear to us that we shouldn't get in the car with our grandfather because he was having trouble remembering things and had a tendency to get lost. Of course, you can guess what happened. I reminded my mom that our grandfather – her dad – asked us to go for a ride, and my sister and I didn't know how to politely decline because we were both younger than 10 years old at the time. So off we went. During the entire ride, my sister and I asked our grandfather if he knew where he was because we were convinced that he was lost.

I told my mom that we were terrified. Then I let that sink in a little bit before telling her that I couldn't let the same thing happen to her – I couldn't let her endanger herself or others. I'm sure it was hard for her to hear that, but she gave up her keys without a fight. I think she was so cooperative because I made it clear that I was looking out for her rather than trying to take away her independence.

You could tell your parents that having a conversation about their finances would be like their gift to you – a gift they likely would have wanted from their parents. Hopefully this will resonate because they won't want you to go through what they endured with their parents.

AGREE ON TRIGGER POINTS

If your parents are resisting your efforts to talk about their finances now, you might be able to get them to agree on possible scenarios when they would be willing to share information with you. Financial psychologist Dr. Mary Gresham[4] recommends saying, "I don't want to take control and deprive you of your freedom and independence." Then ask, "What can we set out as a marker that would say we need to consider X, Y, Z? I want you to tell me when you might be in need of more support. What would need to happen?"

The point is to get your parents thinking about triggering events – such as a stroke, dementia, loss of a spouse – that would require them to get help from you. Ask them to make a list of these situations and give you a copy so you'll know when they need more support than what they're getting now, Gresham said. Point out that by creating this list, you're giving them control. And be sure to refer to it if one of the situations arises to remind your parents that they already agreed to share information with you at this point.

TAKE AN INDIRECT APPROACH

Your parents might not be willing to *tell* you anything about their finances, but they might agree to *write down* the information you're trying to get. You could let them know that you understand that they're reluctant to share personal financial details. However, add that you think it's important for you to have access to this information if a crisis were to arise. Then ask if they'd be willing to make a list of the accounts, insurance policies, legal documents, and final wishes they have. Tell them they can hang onto the list, but they need to tell you where you can find it in case of an emergency.

To make it easy for both you and your parents, I've created a fill-in-the-blank "In Case of Emergency" organizer. You can download it at CameronHuddleston.com for free if you've purchased this book. then give it to your parents. It asks them to provide a variety of information – including financial, health care and personal – that you would need if you have to help care for them or when they die.

This strategy can work well with parents who are reluctant to speak openly about their finances. It lets them maintain control of the information they're giving you. Again, though, it's important that they let you know where you can find their financial inventory if you need it. If they're still wary, ask them to take it a step further by making a list of the situations in which it's okay for you to have access to their financial inventory.

NOTES

1. Daniel Lash, http://www.vlpfa.com/team/daniel-p-lash-cfp-aif (Accessed Jan. 3, 2019).
2. Linda Fodrini-Johnson, https://eldercareanswers.com/about-us/meet-our-founder/ (Accessed Jan. 3, 2019).
3. Brad Klontz, https://www.yourmentalwealth.com/about-us/dr-brad-klontz/ (Accessed Jan. 3, 2019).
4. Mary Gresham, http://doctorgresham.com/ (Accessed Jan. 3, 2019).

15

Getting Through to Reluctant Parents: Success Stories

Some people will read this book, use one of the conversation starters I provided in Chapter 7, and easily get their parents to start sharing details about their finances. For some, it will be a lot tougher.

As I wrote in Chapter 3, there are several reasons parents might be reluctant to talk about money with their kids. You might be thinking, "Lucky me, just about every one of those reasons applies to my parents. How am I ever going to get through to them? Mom changes the subject every time I bring it up, and Dad tells me to mind my own business."

Certainly, if you're getting a lot of pushback, it probably doesn't seem like it's worth the effort to try to have conversations with your parents about their finances. But if you're willing to keep working at it, your efforts might pay off, as they did for Jen and Joel. Both have parents who've made their share of financial mistakes and, for that reason, don't like talking about money. But neither Jen nor Joel wanted to sit by idly and watch their parents struggle financially. So they didn't let their parents' reluctance to talk stop them from trying.

Little by little, Jen and Joel have been able to get their parents to open up about their finances so they can help them take steps to start managing their money better. They both admit that there still is work to be done. But their stories show that there is hope for getting through to even the most reluctant of parents. They also illustrate why it's important to start talking to your parents sooner rather than later because it can take time–in some cases, a lot of time – to make any progress.

JEN's STORY

For Jen, getting her mom to open up about her finances is still a work in progress. It hasn't been easy to get as far as she has, but Jen has been persistent because she knows her mom is struggling and wants to help her get her finances on track before it's too late.

Jen's family never talked about money while she was growing up. "I just assumed my parents were doing okay," she said. "From what I knew, we never had debt, never used credit cards. My parents didn't make a lot of money, but we also didn't do a lot of expensive things."

However, Jen's dad developed cirrhosis – a liver disease – when she was 13 and started receiving disability benefits. When he died in 2006 when Jen was 16, his disability checks stopped coming, and Jen's mom didn't know what to do without that second source of income. "Everything had been right at the brink and they were just making it," she said. That's when everything started going downhill financially for her mom.

Jen knew her mom wasn't making much money and actually didn't work for several months in 2011 and 2012 while she was caring for Jen's grandmother. When Jen moved back home with her mom after finishing graduate school in 2012, she could see that her mom's spending habits were not sustainable. "I knew she couldn't be well off," Jen said. "I knew she couldn't be saving for retirement. I just didn't know the extent of what was going on." She tried to ask, but her mom didn't want to talk about money because she was filled with a lot of guilt and shame, Jen said.

Jen, on the other hand, was taking charge of her finances. She got married in 2015, and both she and her husband were trying to pay off their student loans as fast as possible. Jen even created a blog, ModernFrugality.com,[1] in 2016 to write about how she and her husband were eliminating $78,000 in debt. She would share some of her money-saving strategies with her mom as a way to get her talking about money. Sometimes that worked. "I learned that was a better way to approach it than asking probing questions," Jen said.

While some of her family members were visiting from out of town, Jen was discussing what she and her husband had done to take control of their finances and mentioned that they had read financial guru Dave Ramsey's *The Total Money Makeover* book.[2] A cousin said she had taken one of Ramsey's money courses. So Jen took advantage of that moment to ask her mom if she would like to take Ramsey's nine-week "Financial Peace University" course with her. For years, she had been asking her mom to take the course but never had any luck getting her to agree. But Jen assumed that her mom might be motivated to take the course this time because her cousin, who was doing well financially, was recommending it. "Having it come from somebody else – I'm learning parents don't take lessons from their children well," Jen said. And she was right – her mom agreed to take the class.

"I wanted to take this journey with her and support her in any way that I could," Jen said. But after every class when Jen asked her mom what she thought about what they were being taught, her mom was silent. At the end of the course in November 2016, though, she finally opened up. "She was like, 'I don't feel like I can change any of that stuff. I'm set in my ways. This is who I am,'" Jen said. It led to an emotional outpouring, which made Jen realize that there was a lot more to her mom's financial problems than just money. "I didn't know there was so much behind that," Jen said. "It was really surprising."

However, Jen didn't learn about how bad things really were for her mom until 2017. She and her husband were in the market for their first home, so Jen was spending a lot time looking at real estate listings online. That's when she discovered that her mom's house was listed as a foreclosure. What's worse, it had been in foreclosure for more than 900 days.

"I was like, 'Mom, what's going on?'" Jen said. Her mom said it was a mistake and laughed it off. Jen knew she wasn't going to get any answers then, but she wasn't ready to give up. Within a few months, Jen's mom finally admitted that her house was in foreclosure. Jen helped her have a yard sale and move into an inexpensive one-bedroom apartment. She also encouraged her mom to learn more about the 401(k) retirement plan her employer offered. "She did that and started contributing a portion of her income to her company's 401(k)," Jen said. "She was really proud. I was proud of her, too, and I let her know it was really cool she did that."

However, because her mom has so little saved for retirement, Jen knows that she'll need to work as long as she physically can. But her mom's health issues might make that difficult. So Jen has been offering her mom tips – such as suggestions that she exercise more and eat healthier – so she can improve her health and work longer.

Since taking the money course, Jen's mom has been shopping less and thinking about her purchases more. And she asked Jen for help with making meal plans because Jen has self-published a book on Amazon about the money-saving benefits of meal planning. "I don't think she executed the meal plan, but she did approach me and ask," Jen said.

Despite her mom's progress in some areas, Jen still sees her mom making financial missteps. But rather than criticize her, Jen said she tries to diplomatically offer her suggestions. "I've had to learn to pick my battles more. I used to pick every battle," Jen said. "That just pushed her away. It was more destructive than it was constructive."

Jen also knows that there are a lot more financial conversations she needs to have with her mom – such as whether she has a will or a living will that spells out what sort of medical care she would want if she's unable to decide on her own. "Those conversations are next on our list," she said. Nonetheless, Jen said she feels like she's come a long way in getting her mom to open up, thanks to the money course they took together.

> **LESSON:** It goes to show that getting a third party involved can get a reluctant parent to start talking about their finances (as I wrote in Chapter 14). And Jen's experience shows that offering to help with financial tasks – rather than asking probing questions – can make money conversations easier.

JOEL'S STORY

Joel's parents often argued about money when he was younger. They were struggling because his dad had lost his job and was bouncing from one low-paying job to another. "That led to a lot of financial issues in the household," Joel said. In fact, it got so bad that his parents declared bankruptcy when he was 13.

"That creates a lot of stigma and shame," he said. As a result, money wasn't something his parents wanted to discuss – not even with each other. But Joel said that his parents' bankruptcy taught him a valuable lesson. "I decided after seeing that growing up that I wanted to have my finances buttoned up," he said. "I don't want to have an issue in my marriage like my parents had in theirs just because of money." So he and his wife talk frequently – at least weekly, often daily – about their finances. Joel even shares financial advice with others through his podcast, How to Money.[3] But conversations with his parents have been a struggle.

"When it comes to talking to my parents now about their finances, it's definitely not easy," Joel said. "I would say because of their rocky past with money, it's something you have to handle with great care."

Initially, he didn't handle those conversations with care. Joel admits that when he first started trying to talk with his parents about financial matters when he was in his early 20s and they were in their early 50s, he came on too strong. "I probably turned them away a little bit in the beginning," he said. "I probably wanted to fix all of their finances for them – which is not what anybody wants."

Thinking he knew more about money than his parents did and then trying to correct their mistakes backfired. Joel realizes now that his parents just wanted him to understand and empathize with their struggles, not fix their investing strategy. But it took him a while, he said, "to come down off my high horse and begin to have an honest and caring conversation."

Actually, it took about three to four years for Joel to develop the right approach and get his parents to discuss anything financial. The way he did it was by finding small ways that he could offer to help them. For example, shortly after he got married, Joel had jaw surgery and stayed with his parents for a few days to recover. They got into a conversation about his parents' bank, and he learned that the bank was charging them a monthly maintenance fee of $18 to $20. So he offered to help them switch to another account without a monthly fee. He then offered to help them find other ways to save money, such as cutting the cable cord.

Over time, Joel's been able to expand the conversations from specific bills and ways to save to how his parents think about money and prioritize spending. "It gets into, 'You said you wanted to travel for all these years, but you don't travel. Why is that? Why don't you prioritize that with the money you have?'" he said. "I want to hear what their priorities are. I want to hear what they care about." But Joel said he also wants to be able to help his parents. So when they say that they value something, he asks them if the way they're spending money is aligning with what they value.

Those sorts of questions open the door to better conversations and ways for Joel to offer to help his parents improve their finances. "I know that money has been a huge issue for them over the years," he said. "I know the peace I've had in my marriage because of my relationship with money. I want that for my parents. I see them having a healthier approach to their finances. It's encouraging. I want to see that for them because I know the stranglehold money can have on your life when you use it poorly."

Plus, as selfish as it might seem, Joel said he wants his parents to get their finances in order to make things easier for him and his siblings. "I want them to be prepared because when a parent does pass away and their finances are in shambles, it creates a lot of issues for the kids," he said. "So that's in the back of my mind. But more than anything, I want them to thrive. I want them to have a healthy approach to money because I know how good it's been for me, and I want that for them."

That's why he keeps pushing them – gently – to keep talking about their finances. Sometimes the conversations last just five minutes. Sometimes they talk for 30 minutes or more at the dinner table. And sometimes his parents even come to Joel for advice. Now that they're in their 60s and thinking about retirement, Joel's parents are asking him at what age they should start collecting Social Security benefits (his answer: the longer they wait, the bigger their monthly check will be). His dad has asked whether he should take his pension from his employer as a lump sum or steady payouts over time. Joel talked his mom into increasing her contribution to her retirement plan at work. And when they bought a new house, he talked them into getting a 15-year mortgage instead of a 30-year-mortgage so they wouldn't have to keep making a big monthly payment well into retirement.

Joel said those sorts of conversations wouldn't be possible with his parents if he hadn't spent years getting them comfortable discussing money matters. You can't just ask your parents out of the blue to share details about their finances and expect them to open up. "You can only get answers to those questions if you've invested the time," Joel said.

There's a lot more Joel would like to discuss with his parents about their finances. "But I'm trying to walk that healthy balance of not being a nag and not pissing my parents off because I love them very much," he said. At least, the conversation pathways are open, he said. "We're able to have a back-and-forth, a discussion."

> **LESSON: Don't come on too strong with reluctant parents. Invest the time to get them comfortable talking about money matters.**

NOTES

1. ModernFrugality.com, https://www.modernfrugality.com/about-me/ (Accessed Jan. 3, 2019).

2. Dave Ramsey, *The Total Money Makeover: A Proven Plan for Financial Fitness* (Nashville, TN: Thomas Nelson, 2013).

3. How to Money, https://www.howtomoney.com/about-us/ (Accessed Jan. 3, 2019).

16

What to Do If Your Parents Won't Talk

Elise has tried time and again to talk with her mom about her finances because she's worried that her mom won't be able to support herself in retirement. Her mother has owned a small retail business for more than 40 years, but it wasn't doing well in the early 2010s. In fact, she had talked her second husband, Elise's stepfather, into borrowing against their home to help to support the business. On top of that, Elise's mom got pneumonia and had to be put into a medically induced coma. "She came out of it as okay as you can be, but she will never be the healthy person she was," said Elise, who asked not to use her real name to protect her family's privacy. "One of the casualties was her business. It completely fell apart."

However, having to close the business wasn't the only financial problem. "My mom has never been good with money, which I didn't understand until I got older," Elise said. "She came from money. My grandparents were quite wealthy. My mom thought of herself as an heiress, so she didn't save." Elise knows that her mom inherited money from her mother when she died in 2002. But the money is in a trust, and Elise has no idea how much is in there. She's tried to talk to her mom about whether she'll be able to support herself in retirement, but her mom shuts down any kind of conversation Elise tries to have with her about money. "I know she'd be more open if she felt more confident in her finances," Elise said. "It's the fact that she needs help that makes it so difficult to talk to her."

Because she knows her mom likely won't open up about where she stands financially, Emily has taken matters into her own hands. She's been funding a savings account for her mom. "I'm planning ahead in case there's a big problem but hoping for the best," she said.

Despite your best efforts, your parents might never be comfortable sharing information about their finances with you. You could try every conversation starter and tactic I've suggested in this book, but they will continue to balk because of some deep-seated conviction against – or fear of – talking about money. That's when it's time to come up with Plan B, as Elise did.

MAKE A LAST-DITCH ATTEMPT TO GET SOME INFORMATION

If your parents have shot down your attempts to talk time and again, ask if they at least can let you know whether they have any estate planning documents such as a will, power of attorney, or advance directive or if they can give you the name of any financial professional they might have hired. Financial psychologist Brad Klontz[1] recommends saying something like, "If you're not comfortable talking to us, if you got in a car wreck, who would we contact – your attorney, your accountant?"

If there's nobody to contact and your parents don't have any estate planning documents, consider offering to pay in part or in full to have an attorney draft these documents for them. Let your parents know that you don't have to see the documents but emphasize how important they are to prevent family feuds and financial disasters when they die or if they become incapacitated. You can play detective to get the information you need if you have to settle their estate when they die or if they can no longer make financial or health care decisions on their own. But neither you nor anyone else will have the legal authority to handle their finances without power of attorney – which means someone will have to go through the lengthy and expensive process of getting conservatorship.

DECIDE WHAT YOU'RE WILLING AND ABLE TO DO

Even if your parents aren't willing to share any information about their finances with you, there is a chance that they might want your help someday. That's why **you need to get very clear** *now* **on what you're willing and able to do**, said Josh Nelson,[2] a certified financial planner and founder of Keystone Financial Services. "If you're clear in advance, you won't be so emotional when it comes up," he said. "People don't tend to make good financial decisions in a highly emotional state."

Jen, whose story I shared in Chapter 15, has offered her mom advice on how to improve her finances. But Jen and her husband have decided not to provide Jen's mom with any financial assistance at this point "for our sake and for her dignity," Jen said. She recognizes that her mom's financial mistakes aren't her own, and she doesn't have to feel guilty for that – even if her mom ever tries to lay a guilt trip on her. Jen said it's important to establish boundaries to protect yourself emotionally and financially.

You might decide that you want to start setting aside money to help your parents, or stay in your current home rather than downsizing once the kids leave so Mom or Dad could move in. You might decide that you can't or don't want to provide financial support but can help provide physical care for them. Or you might decide that you can't help them at all. The decision is yours. However, you do need to let your siblings know what you're in a position to do so they can plan accordingly, Nelson said.

MAKE A PLAN WITH YOUR SIBLINGS

Even if your parents won't talk about their finances, you and your siblings need to talk. Nelson said you should have a conversation about what roles each of you will play and how you can chip in if your parents need help. "Even in the best of circumstances, it can create friction in the family if conversations haven't come up and siblings have different ideas about care," Nelson said.

I wrote in Chapter 5 about getting on the same page with your siblings before talking to your parents. Many of those tips are still applicable for talking with your siblings if your parents refuse to talk with you about their finances. Take the time to read – or reread – that chapter for help navigating conversations with your siblings about your parents' money and well-being.

Ideally, you shouldn't just talk to your siblings about who will do what. You should develop a complete plan of action. For example, if one of you has agreed to care for your parents if they have health needs and will have to give up a job to do so, the other siblings should determine if they can provide financial support to that sibling – and, if so, how much. Or all of you might agree to set up an emergency fund for your parents because none of you will have access to their bank accounts if your parents haven't named any of you power of attorney. You could open a savings account and each make monthly contributions to it so there's cash to cover your parents bills while you go through the legal process of becoming conservator.

You should also discuss end-of-life care for your parents. If your parents don't have living wills that spell out what sort of medical treatment they would want, ideally you and your siblings should agree whether to keep your parents on life support before your parents are in a situation where that decision needs to be made. Having these discussions and hammering out details such as this beforehand can help avoid family fighting when emergencies arise.

If one or all of your siblings don't want to get involved, keep them updated on what you're doing if you have to care for your parents financially or physically. You don't want to give them any reason to think you're keeping secrets from them or mishandling your parents' money.

FOCUS ON YOUR FINANCES

Your parents gave you a home to grow up in, fed you, and put clothes on your back. They might have bought you your first car, put you through college, let you move back in when you couldn't get a job, paid for your wedding, or even helped you buy your first home. Now you feel like you owe them if they ever need your help. But you shouldn't sacrifice your own financial security to help your parents, said John Cooper,[3] a certified financial planner with Greenwood Capital.

"I tell my clients to think of it in context of you love your parents and want to do all you can. You have an important role to play. But you really have to make sure your finances are in order first – your retirement, kids' college," Cooper said. "As difficult as it sounds, you have to put your priorities first. You'll have to pay for those things and will get no assistance."

So before worrying about Mom or Dad, get on top of your own finances. Figure out what you want and need to do – whether it's paying off debt, saving more each month so you can retire comfortably, building an emergency fund to cover unexpected expenses, or saving for your kids' college education.

You might find that you can reach your own financial goals and be able to afford to help your parents. It's something you need to plan for, though, rather than try to figure out as you go. For example, although Jen isn't currently helping her mom out financially, she is saving money in case her mom needs long-term care. "We're doing what we can without sacrificing our own well-being," she said. Elise, who's worried about whether her mom can support herself in retirement, is doing the same.

If you don't plan, you really could put your own financial well-being at risk by supporting your parents. Then that could force your children into the same situation where they will have to choose whether to sacrifice their well-being to help support you. You don't want them to feel like they have to make that choice, do you?

Consider meeting with a financial planner for help with your finances. You can search for one near you at GuideVine .com, a free service that helps connect people with prescreened financial advisers who are fiduciaries (which means they're legally required to work in clients' best interests). You can also find a certified financial planner through the Financial Planning Association's Plannersearch.org website and the National Association of Personal Financial Advisors' website, NAPFA.org. There are financial planners who charge by the hour, so it might not cost you much to meet a couple of times to draft a financial plan.

If you can't – or don't want to – pay for financial advice, there are plenty of free resources. Your bank's website might have articles and information about personal finance, as might your workplace retirement plan's website. The Consumer Financial Protection Bureau's website, Consumerfinance .gov, has a wealth of information on a variety of money topics. And there are plenty of websites dedicated to personal finance – including Kiplinger.com, Money.com, Investopedia .com, Bankrate.com, GOBankingRates.com, and NerdWallet .com. If you spend time increasing your own knowledge of personal finance, you'll likely feel more comfortable helping your parents with their finances if they run into trouble.

PARENTS WITH DEMENTIA

If your parents refuse to share information about their finances but have dementia or some other cognitive impairment, you will have to step in if you want to protect them from financial – and physical – ruin. That doesn't mean you should just jump in and take over, at least not initially. Offer to set up automatic bill pay for them or help with other financial tasks so they can have more time to do things they enjoy. Help them get free copies of their credit report at Annualcreditreport.com, then suggest that you go through the report together to look for signs that they're victims of fraud – such as accounts they didn't open. If you can find ways to start inserting yourself into your parents' financial lives, you might be able to gather information about their accounts, check for signs that they're being scammed, and ensure that they're managing their money wisely. The goal is to help them make decisions, then take over more control – with their best interests in mind – as their abilities decline.

If they resist all of your efforts, then you might have to be sneaky to gather the information you need to help and protect your parents. For example, you might want to remove credit cards from their wallet and replace them with a secured credit card, which requires a deposit that becomes the spending limit and will help prevent them from charging more than they can afford to pay. You might have to go through their mail to intercept donation requests, sweepstakes entry forms, and other solicitations for cash. Or you might need to start pointing out the financial mistakes they're making as a result of memory loss – in a caring, not condescending, way – and let them know that you want to protect them. To do that, tell them they will have to start working with you rather than resisting your efforts to help.

You'll be able to make financial decisions and transactions for them if they've designated you as power of attorney. However, you have to have the actual legal document. Without it, no financial institution will simply take your word that you are power of attorney for your parents. If your parents are unwilling to tell you where their POA documents are but clearly can no longer manage their finances on their own, start searching for them in their home. If you know who their attorney is, call to explain the situation and ask if he or she has your parents' POA documents on file. Most attorneys only keep copies of clients' documents, but they might have an original copy. However, they might not be willing to give it to you unless you can prove that your parent is no longer competent.

If your parents have not designated a power of attorney, you likely will have to go to court to get conservatorship – the legal right to manage your parent's finances (which I explained in Chapter 4). It can be an expensive and lengthy process that will require proving that your parents are no longer competent to manage their financial affairs themselves. If you are appointed conservator, you'll have to file annual reports with the court to show how you are managing your parents' finances.

The Consumer Financial Protection Bureau has a guide to managing someone else's money that could offer you more assistance in figuring out how to help your parents with their finances at https://www.consumerfinance.gov/consumer-tools/managing-someone-elses-money/. Eldercare.gov and the Alzheimer's Association (www.alz.org) also have resources for caregivers.

I'm not going to lie: It's tough to manage your parents' finances if they have memory loss or a condition that leaves them unable to handle money matters on their own. But without help – which they might initially resist – they could make disastrous financial mistakes or become victims of fraud and end up with no money.

LET GO OF GUILT

As I said, it *is* up to you to decide whether you want to help your parents and what level of involvement you want to have. If you have tried and tried to get your parents to share details of their finances, prepare legal documents, and get a handle on their money but they've resisted, you have to accept that there's only so much you can do. It's not up to you to fix your parents' money mistakes by jeopardizing your own financial (or emotional) well-being. It might be time to give yourself permission to let go.

NOTES

1. Brad Klontz, https://www.yourmentalwealth.com/about-us/dr-brad-klontz/ (Accessed Jan. 3, 2019).
2. Josh Nelson, http://www.keystonefinancial.com/team-members/josh-nelson/ (Accessed Jan. 3, 2019).
3. John Cooper, http://wealth.greenwoodcapital.com/our-team/john-w-cooper-cfp (Accessed Jan. 3, 2019).

Pay It Forward: Start Talking to Your Kids

Clearly, you bought this book because you recognize the importance of talking to your parents about their financial situation and their wishes for how their finances should be handled when they're no longer able to handle them on their own. But have you started talking to your kids about your own finances? Are money conversations happening in your house? Are you taking steps to secure your finances so your kids don't have to jeopardize theirs to help you someday?

A survey by Ameriprise found that even though a majority of baby boomers are talking to their parents about financial matters, they're not always having those same conversations with their children.[1] Often, the excuse is that they haven't gotten around to it or haven't thought about it, according to the survey. You can probably relate to that. We all can, actually, because we get so busy keeping up with what we have to do to get through the day that we forget to take time to plan for the future. Before you know it, though, you'll be in a situation where you need your kids' help, but they won't be able to step in because you haven't given them any insight into your finances. That's why you shouldn't wait to start having financial conversations with your kids.

I'm not suggesting that you share every detail about your financial situation, especially if your children still are young. But there are things you should be discussing with them to avoid financial surprises down the road. More importantly, there are things you should be doing to safeguard your finances so you'll never become a burden on your children.

MAKE SURE YOU HAVE ESTATE PLANNING DOCUMENTS

I can't tell you how many times I've heard from my friends that they've been meaning to get around to writing a will. (Yes, the subject does come up when you're a personal finance writer and people frequently pick your brain about money matters.) Most are in their late 30s or 40s and still have kids at home, which is why I tend to tell them they can't put off writing a will another day. If you die without a will, a judge decides who gets what – and that includes your kids.

A will lets you name a guardian for your minor children. It also lets you name someone to manage any assets you leave behind for your children. I know from experience that many parents put off writing a will because they don't know whom to name as guardian. It can be a tough choice to make. But wouldn't you rather make that choice than let a judge who never met you and doesn't know your values make that decision?

Even if your kids are grown, you still need a will or trust to let your wishes be known and to prevent family fights over who gets what. No matter how well you think your kids might get along, every estate planning attorney I know says it's surprising what people will argue about when things are being sorted out after someone dies. "I have a family fighting tooth and nail over reimbursement for one child who mowed a yard for year," said attorney Josh Berkley.

Take time today to schedule a meeting with an attorney to draft a will or living trust so you can have a say in who gets what, even if you don't have a lot. While you're there, have power of attorney and advance health care directive documents drafted, too. You don't necessarily have to give your children financial and health care powers of attorney for you. Just make sure you designate someone you trust. Be sure, though, to let your children know that you've had these documents drafted and where they are stored. It could cost you a few hundred dollars to more than $1,000 to have estate planning documents drafted, depending on how complicated your situation is. But it will definitely be money well spent because these documents will spare your children the financial and emotional turmoil they'll face if you die without a will, slip into a coma without a living will or develop dementia without designating a power or attorney first.

Also make sure you have designated beneficiaries on any life insurance policies and retirement accounts you have. By naming beneficiaries, the money will go directly to them when you die rather than through the probate process that is used to settle estates.

MAKE SAVING FOR RETIREMENT A PRIORITY

Many baby boomers and Gen Xers are putting their own financial security at risk because they're being too generous with their children. A study by Merrill Lynch and Age Wave found that parents are providing **$500 billion in support every year** to their 18- to 34-year-old adult children.[2] They're paying for everything from student loans to food and groceries to cell phone bills and rent. **In fact,** nearly three-quarters of parents say they have put their children's interests ahead of their own need to save for retirement, according to the study.

As parents, we need to support our children. But there comes a point when we have to cut them off for their own financial well-being and for ours. If you've been supporting your kids instead of saving for your retirement, you could be dependent on them for financial support as you age. You probably don't want that. And your kids might not be prepared to help out if they don't have their own financial act together after years of relying on the Bank of Mom and Dad.

So it might be time for you to have a conversation with your children if you've been putting your own financial security at risk to help them. They might not even realize that you're making sacrifices to help them. But if you make it clear that you need to focus more on saving for retirement so you don't have to move into their basement someday, they'll probably get the clue pretty quickly that they need to stop relying on you for handouts.

You might never need to even have this conversation if your kids are young and you start prioritizing saving for retirement now. Financial planners typically recommend saving at least 10 percent to 15 percent of your income annually to have enough for a comfortable retirement. But that assumes that you start saving that much in your 20s and don't retire until your 60s. Use a retirement calculator to get a better idea of how much you need to save based on your current age and how much income you'll likely need in retirement. Your workplace retirement plan might offer a calculator you can use, or there are plenty of them online. Investment firms such as Fidelity and Vanguard have free retirement calculators on their websites. NewRetirement .com has a variety of retirement calculators. And OnTrajectory .com offers a more in-depth analysis of your retirement needs for a fee.

If you're deciding whether to save for your kids' college or your retirement, choose the latter. There are no loans for retirement, but there are for college. You might not want your kids to be saddled with student loan debt when they graduate. However, keep in mind that they'll have a lot more time at that point to pay off what they owe than you will have to save for retirement.

Take advantage of your workplace retirement plan if your employer offers one. Contributing to a 401(k), 403(b) or 457 is the easiest way to save for retirement because contributions can be deducted automatically from your paycheck, and the money comes out before taxes (which lowers your taxable income). Plus, plenty of employers match employee contributions to workplace retirement accounts. The most common match is a dollar-for-dollar match, with a majority of companies requiring employees to contribute at least 6 percent of their income to a 401(k) to get the full matching contribution.[3] So if your employer offers matching contributions and you're not contributing enough to get the full match, you're giving up free money for retirement.

If your employer doesn't offer a workplace retirement plan, you can open an individual retirement account – either an IRA or Roth IRA – at a low-fee investment firm such as Charles Schwab, Fidelity, or Vanguard. If you're self-employed, you could save for retirement in a solo 401(k), SEP IRA, or SIMPLE IRA – as well as a traditional IRA or Roth IRA.

PREPARE FOR LONG-TERM CARE NEEDS

The biggest mistake you can make when it comes to long-term care is not planning for it. There's a good chance you or your spouse (or partner) will need long-term care because a physical or mental health issue will leave you unable to care for yourself. About 70 percent of adults 65 and older will need long-term care at some point, and more than half will need a high level of care for more than 90 days, according to the Bipartisan Policy Center.[4]

I know it's a downer thinking that someday someone might have to help you do things such as driving to the grocery store, taking your medicine on time, making sure your bills get paid, or even going to the bathroom. But ignoring the possibility that you might need help in the future won't prevent it from becoming a reality. It simply means that you and your family won't be prepared, which could wipe out both you and your kids financially. That's because long-term care is expensive.

The cost of professional care can range from about $4,000 a month for a home health aide or assisted living to more than $8,000 a month for a private room in a skilled nursing facility, according to figures from the 2018 Genworth Cost of Care Survey.[5] Of course, you could pay for care out of your own pocket – if you have a lot of money, that is. Or you could limit your out-of-pocket costs by getting **a long-term care insurance policy**. Typically, the younger you are when you sign up, the lower your premium (the cost of the policy) will be. The cost also depends on the amount of the benefit you want, your health when you apply, and the insurer you choose, because rates vary greatly from company to company. For example, the American Association for Long-Term Care found that the annual premium could range from $835 to $2,196 for a policy with a $164,000 benefit for a 55-year-old man.[6] That's why it's important to work with an insurance broker who represents several companies and can help compare prices for you. You can get free quotes from American Association for Long-Term Care members at www.aaltci.org or by calling 818-597-3227.

You don't have to buy a policy with a benefit to cover the entire cost of care, which could make premiums unaffordable. Instead, think about the sources of income you will have that could help pay for care – such as Social Security benefits or a pension – then buy enough insurance to cover the gap. For example, if you get a monthly Social Security check of $2,000 and the cost of assisted living in your area is $4,000 a month, you only need to be able to insure about $2,000 worth of costs each month. To figure out how much coverage you need, you can use Genworth's Cost of Care calculator at https://www.genworth.com/aging-and-you/finances/cost-of-care.html to find out the median costs of various types of care in your area. Genworth also has a calculator to estimate your long-term-care insurance costs.

To take advantage of good health discounts, you can keep down the cost of long-term care insurance by applying when you're younger (in your late 40s or early 50s) when your health is good. Just like with auto and home-owners insurance, you can reduce your premium by opting for a higher deductible, or an elimination period. The longer the elimination period – the number of days you pay out of pocket before coverage kicks in – the lower your premium.[7] You also could save by opting for a defined benefit period that provides coverage for a limited number of years rather than an unlimited benefit period. A policy with a five-year benefit period can cost up to 27 percent less than an unlimited benefit policy, according to the American Association for Long-Term Care. Couples can cut costs by opting for shared benefits, which is basically a pool of money either or both can draw from for care. However, don't try to save money by getting a policy without inflation protection. This will add to the cost but it will ensure that the value of your benefits keep pace with the rising cost of care.

Another option to consider is a **hybrid life insurance policy** that provides a long-term care benefit.[8] These are whole or universal life insurance policies, which means they offer permanent coverage rather than term coverage for a certain number of years. But they include what is called a rider that lets you draw from your death benefits (the amount that would be paid to beneficiaries) to pay for long-term care. If the long-term care benefit is never used, the life insurance policy will pay out on your death – which is appealing if you don't like the idea of paying for a long-term care policy that you might never need. However, you typically have to pay one large up-front premium of $50,000 or more,[9] although some companies allow you to pay premiums over a certain number of years. And the benefit payouts for long-term care tend to be more limited than the benefits from a traditional long-term care insurance policy.[10]

If you have cash on hand, you also could invest in a **long-term care annuity.** You make a lump-sum payment in return for a guaranteed stream of income over a specified period of time. The money you invest goes into two funds – one for long-term care and one for general use. The benefits are that you can use the annuity as a source of income even if you don't need the long-term care benefit. However, the annuity payout might not be enough to pay for long-term care if you need it.[11]

There are government programs that help cover the cost of long-term care, as I wrote in Chapter 12. Medicare does not pay for most long-term care services – typically just short-term care in a nursing facility after hospitalization.[12] Medicaid does cover long-term care at home and in skilled nursing facilities – but typically not in assisted living facilities. To be eligible, though, your income and assets can't exceed certain levels, which are determined by your state.[13] The Department of Veterans Affairs also pays for long-term care services for low-income veterans.[14]

Of course, you could do what most Americans do when it comes to long-term care – rely on family members for help. If you expect to get care from your children, be aware that this could put a huge financial strain on them. Because caregiving can be a full-time job, your kids might have to give up their paying jobs to help you. If you see your children as your only option for care, you need to talk with them sooner rather than later. This will give them time to prepare their own finances. And it will give you time to come up with Plan B if they tell you that they won't be able to care for you.

CREATE YOUR OWN FINANCIAL INVENTORY

You should have your own list of all of the financial information I suggested in Chapter 9 that you gather from your parents. You could use the "In Case of Emergency" organizer available at CameronHuddleston.com. Or you could create your own file.

You don't have to hand over this list to your children now. Just keep it updated and make sure your children – or the person you named in your will as your children's guardian – know where to find it. It will save them the headache of trying to dig up this information on their own if something happens to you and will make it easier for them to help you if you need it.

SCHEDULE A TIME TO TALK ... AND KEEP THE CONVERSATION GOING

If you keep telling yourself you'll get around to having "the talk" with your kids, make sure it actually happens by scheduling a time to sit down and chat. If you don't often talk about money matters in your family, your children might find it a little odd that you want to meet with them to discuss your finances. But you can quickly quash any worries they might have that something's wrong by assuring them that you simply want everyone get on the same page so there are no surprises as you head into retirement or as you age. Here are some things to consider discussing:

Talk about your plans for retirement. If you have a financial plan, don't just tell your kids that everything is covered. Clue them in to the type of lifestyle you plan to have in retirement – whether you'll continue to live in your home, whether you'll relocate, whether you'll be traveling most of the time, or whether you'll be volunteering most days. Why? Because if your kids have children of their own or are planning to start a family, they might have it in their heads that you'll be helping out with childcare. If that's not at all part of your plan, your children need to know. They also might need time to adjust to the idea that you're selling the family home. Talking about your plans might help your children with their own financial planning or simply assure them that you'll be okay in retirement.

If you're not sure yet how you'll support yourself in retirement, your children need to know whether you might need their help in any way. If you delay this conversation out of embarrassment, you'll only make it more difficult for your children. That's because they will have less time to prepare their own finances and make adjustments to help you. You also need to know what level of support they can provide. They might not have the means – or, as harsh as this might sound, the desire – to chip in, which means you need a Plan B.

Talk about where you want to live as you age. As I wrote in Chapter 13, most people don't want to move as they age. If it's important for you to stay in your home even if your health declines, let your children know this. However, you need to take steps to make this possible. That might mean saving enough to cover the cost of retrofitting your home to make it more senior friendly. It might mean getting a long-term care insurance policy to cover the cost of in-home care. It does not mean counting on your kids to put their careers and families on hold to help you age in place.

If you're not determined to stay in your home, let your children know this. It will lift a huge burden from them if they know it's okay to move you to a facility where you can get the care you need. In fact, you might want to scout out senior living facilities where you'd be willing receive care and give your kids a list of the ones that get your stamp of approval.

Talk about your final wishes. No matter how much you – and your kids – don't want to have to think about your death, it will happen. You can make it easier for those you leave behind by letting them know your final wishes so there's no question about what you want. I've already told my children (who still are relatively young) that I want to be cremated and that they can choose where to spread my ashes. My husband wants to be cremated and have his ashes planted with a tree. I've found that talking openly about it removes the stigma about death and the sense of dread that it will happen someday. I'm so grateful my mom had these conversations with me before she developed Alzheimer's. I even know what type of service she wants.

Let your children know whether you want to be buried, cremated, or even donated to science. Tell them what type of service you want, whether there are particular readings or songs you prefer. Then put it all in writing so there is no question about what you want when the time comes.

Most importantly, these conversations should be ongoing. Keeping your children updated on your situation will help all of you develop plans to address issues as you age. And it will give your children peace of mind knowing that if they ever need to help you, they will be able to because you've shared with them the information they need.

NOTES

1. Ameriprise Financial (2007), "Ameriprise Financial Money Across Generations Study Reveals Finances Still a Taboo Topic at the Family Dinner Table," https://www.businesswire.com/news/home/20071115006123/en/Ameriprise-Financial-Money-Generations-SM-Study-Reveals (Accessed Jan. 3, 2019).

2. Merrill Lynch and Age Wave (2018), "Parents Spend Twice as Much on Their Adult Children as They Save for Retirement Merrill Lynch Study Finds," https://newsroom.bankofamerica.com/press-releases/global-wealth-and-investment-management/parents-spend-twice-much-their-adult (Accessed Jan. 3, 2019).

3. Stephen Miller, Society for Human Resource Management (2015), "Dollar-for-Dollar Is Now Most Common 401(k) Match," https://www.shrm.org/resourcesandtools/hr-topics/benefits/pages/bigger-401k-matches.aspx (Accessed Jan. 3, 2019).

4. Bipartisan Policy Center (2017), "Financing Long-Term Services and Supports: Seeking Bipartisan Solutions in Politically Challenging Times," https://bipartisanpolicy.org/wp-content/uploads/2017/07/BPC-Health-Financing-Long-Term-Services-and-Supports.pdf (Accessed Jan. 3, 2019).

5. Genworth (2018), "2018 Cost of Care Survey," https://www.genworth .com/aging-and-you/finances/cost-of-care.html (Accessed Jan. 3, 2019).

6. Jesse Sloam, American Association for Long-Term Care Insurance, "How Much Does Long-Term Care Insurance Cost? Here Are Costs for 2018 for Leading Long-Term Care Insurers," http://www.aaltci.org/long-term-care-insurance/learning-center/long-term-care-insurance-costs-2015.php (Accessed Jan. 3, 2019).

7. American Association for Long-Term Care Insurance, "Long-Term Care Insurance: There Are Simple Ways to Reduce the Cost," http://www .aaltci.org/long-term-care-insurance/learning-center/ways-to-save.php (Accessed Jan. 3, 2019).

8. Elder Law Answers (2018), "Hybrid Policies Allow You to Have Your Long-Term Care Insurance Cake and Eat It, Too," https://www.elderlaw answers.com/hybrid-policies-allow-you-to-have-your-long-term-care-insurance-cake-and-eat-it-too-15541 (Accessed Jan. 3, 2019).

9. American Association for Long-Term Care Insurance, "Compare Life Insurance Policies That Pay for Long Term Care," http://www.aaltci .org/long-term-care-insurance/learning-center/life-insurance-ltc-benefits.php (Accessed Jan. 3, 2019).

10. LongTermCare.gov, "Using Life Insurance to Pay for Long-Term Care," https://longtermcare.acl.gov/costs-how-to-pay/using-life-insurance-to-pay-for-long-term-care.html (Accessed Jan. 3, 2019).

11. LongTermCare.gov, "Annuities," https://longtermcare.acl.gov/costs-how-to-pay/paying-privately/annuities.html (Accessed Jan. 3, 2019).

12. LongTermCare.gov, "Medicare," https://longtermcare.acl.gov/medicare-medicaid-more/medicare.html (Accessed Jan. 3, 2019).

13. LongTermCare.gov, "Financial Requirements," https://longtermcare .acl.gov/medicare-medicaid-more/medicaid/medicaid-eligibility/finan cial-requirements.html (Accessed Jan. 3, 2019).

14. LongTermCare.gov, "Veterans Affairs Benefits," https://longtermcare.acl .gov/medicare-medicaid-more/veterans-affairs-benefits.html (Accessed Jan. 3, 2019).

A Final Note

As I wrote in Chapter 2, talking to your parents sooner rather than later will give you peace of mind. Then you can *spend the time you do have* with your parents without that nagging feeling that you're not prepared to give them the help they might someday need. I would also encourage you to spend time listening to your parents' stories and recording them. I know this has nothing to do with personal finance, but it is something you will value greatly when your parents are no longer with you.

My father died before any of my children were born. So they never got the chance to hear all of the great stories he would tell me about his childhood. I've tried to share those stories, but I don't really do them justice. I also share the stories my mom told me about her childhood with my children, but it's not the same as hearing her tell them – which she hasn't been able to do. My oldest daughter is my only child who knew my mom before she started losing her memory.

I wish I could go back and record my parents telling those stories even more than I wish I could go back and have better conversations with my mom and dad about their finances. Fortunately, I saw the need to start talking to my mom about money matters – not all aspects of her finances, but at least some – before it was too late. Encouraging her to update her essential legal documents while she still was competent made it possible for me to help manage her finances and get her the care she has needed as her Alzheimer's has progressed. I have no regrets there.

Trust me, you won't regret talking to your parents about their finances if it makes it easier for you to help them someday, too. Let them know that having conversations with you about their finances will be as much of a gift as sharing their stories so you can hang onto those memories and pass them down. Don't wait. Start talking today.

Additional Resources

I've tried to be thorough in this book by providing as much detail as possible about the financial topics you need to discuss with your parents. However, entire books could be written about estate planning, retirement planning, long-term care, and managing aging parents' finances. If you want to dig deeper and gather more information, there are other books and online resources that can help.

In this appendix, I've also included all of the resources I mentioned throughout the book. Think of it as a one-stop guide to personal finance resources that you can refer to again and again as you talk with your parents and help them with their finances.

ADDITIONAL READING

Chast, Roz. *Can't We Talk About Something More Pleasant?* Bloomsbury USA, 2013.

Morris, Virginia. *How to Care for Aging Parents: A One-Stop Resource for All Your Medical, Financial, Housing, and Emotional Issues.* Workman Publishing, 2014.

Opdyke, Jeff. *Protecting Your Parents' Money: The Essential Guide to Helping Mom and Dad Navigate the Finances of Retirement.* HarperBusiness 2011.

Sackler, Lori. *The M Word: The Money Talk Every Family Needs to Have About Wealth and Their Financial Future.* McGraw-Hill Education, 2013.

Taylor, Dan. *The Parent Care Conversation: 6 Strategies for Dealing with the Emotional and Financial Challenges of Aging Parents.* Penguin Books, 2006.

AGING ISSUES AND ASSISTANCE FOR ELDERS

- AARP: This advocacy group for adults 50 and older has lots of free articles and resources to help with financial matters at https://www.aarp.org.
- Eldercare Locator: This public service of the U.S. Administration on Aging helps connect older adults with local support services and provides resources for caregivers at https://eldercare.acl.gov/Public/Index.aspx.
- National Council on Aging: This organization has a wealth of information on its website, https://www.ncoa .org/, to help older adults stay economically secure as they age. Its free BenefitsCheckUp service at https:// www.benefitscheckup.org/ helps seniors find out what benefit programs they might be eligible for to save money on health care, medication, food, housing, utilities, and more. If your parents are struggling financially, this site can point you or them to resources that can help.
- National Asian Pacific Center on Aging: This organization collaborates with mainstream aging associations to provide support services for older Asian American and Pacific Islander adults at https://www.napca.org/.
- National Caucus and Center on Black Aging: This organization is dedicated to minority and low-income aging issues. It provides employment, health and wellness, and affordable housing services at https://www.ncba-aged .org/.
- National Hispanic Council on Aging: This organization provides programs to meet the needs of Hispanic older adults at https://www.nhcoa.org/.
- SAGE: This national advocacy group for LGBT elders has a variety of resources on topics ranging from legal and financial matters to housing to aging at https://www .sageusa.org/.
- Senior Service America: This nonprofit organization operates the Senior Community Service Employment Program and other programs for older workers. Information about its programs is available at http://www .seniorserviceamerica.org/.

- The Scan Foundation: This charity that promotes aging with dignity offers a "10 Things You Should Know" series of guides to help aging adults and family members at https://www.thescanfoundation.org/publications/10-things.

CREDIT AND DEBT

- AnnualCreditReport.com: This is the official site directed by federal law to provide free credit reports. Consumers can get copies of their credit reports from each of the three credit reporting agencies once a year at https://www.annualcreditreport.com/. Credit reports include the lines of credit a person has (credit cards, mortgages, consumer loans, etc.), amounts owed, and payment history.
- MyFICO.com: This is the consumer education website of Fair Isaac Corp., the creator of the FICO credit score. Consumers can learn about FICO credit scores – which are the scores most commonly used by lenders – and get their score for a fee at https://www.myfico.com/.
- National Foundation for Credit Counseling: This non-profit financial counseling organization has a network of member agencies serving all 50 states. If your parents are struggling with debt, they can get free or low-cost credit and debt counseling from NFCC member agencies by calling 800-388-2227 or using the NFCC counselor locator online at https://www.nfcc.org/locator/.

DEATH AND END-OF-LIFE

- Aging with Dignity: This nonprofit organization provides resources to help families discuss advance care planning and end-of-life wishes. At its Five Wishes website, https://fivewishes.org/, it sells a conversation guide about advance planning and a Five Wishes advance directive document that allows people to detail their end-of-life medical, personal, emotional, and spiritual needs.

- CaringInfo: This website of the National Hospice and Palliative Care Organization provides free resources to help people make decisions about end-of-life care and services at http://www.caringinfo.org/.
- Compassion & Choices: This organization offers a Plan Your Care Resource Center at https://compassionand choices.org/end-of-life-planning/ to help people navigate end-of-life choices.

ESTATE PLANNING

- American Bar Association: If your parents have limited financial resources, they might be able to get free legal help through the American Bar Association's Find Legal Help website at http://www.findlegalhelp.org.
- Avvo: This free database allows you to search for attorneys by practice area or name and state at https://www.avvo .com/.
- National Academy of Elder Law Attorneys: This is an association of attorneys who specialize in elder law and special needs planning. It has a searchable directory at https:// www.naela.org/findlawyer.
- National Association of Estate Planners and Council: This is an association of financial and legal professionals who are Accredited Estate Planners and Estate Planning Law Specialists. It has a searchable database of members at http://www.naepc.org/designations/estate-planners/ search#spec/All.
- Nolo: This publisher of do-it-yourself legal guides sells estate planning documents and has free resources on estate planning at https://www.nolo.com/.
- LegalZoom: This company provides both DIY estate planning documents and access to legal help at https://www .legalzoom.com/.
- RocketLawyer: This website sells customizable legal documents and provides access to attorneys at https://www .rocketlawyer.com/.

FINANCIAL PLANNING

- AARP Financial Advisor Interview Guide: This free tool provides questions to ask an advisor before hiring one and tips to start a conversation at https://campaigns.aarp .org/interviewanadvisor.
- American Association of Daily Money Managers: Some members of this organization volunteer their services to help low-income people with money management. The association's website has a list of state agencies that provide daily money management services at https://secure .aadmm.com/state-agencies/.
- American Institute of CPAs: This association representing the accounting profession has a Find a CPA tool at https://www.aicpa.org/forthepublic/findacpa.html.
- Broker Check: This free tool from the Financial Industry Regulatory Authority (FINRA) lets you research the background of financial advisers, brokers, and firms at https://brokercheck.finra.org/.
- Financial Planning Association: This association of certified financial planner professionals has a searchable database of members at http://www.plannersearch.org/.
- GuideVine: This free service connects people with prescreened financial advisers at https://www.guidevine .com/.
- National Association of Personal Financial Advisors: This association of fee-only financial advisors has a searchable database of members at https://www.napfa.org/find-an-advisor.

GOVERNMENT AGENCIES AND BENEFITS

- Benefits.gov: Rather than scour countless government websites, your parents can visit https://www.benefits .gov/ to find out which government benefit programs they might be eligible for – including financial benefits, housing assistance, health care and medical assistance, and Social Security and retirement.

- Medicaid: If your parents' income is low enough, they might qualify for Medicaid coverage for long-term care at home or in a nursing home. Information about the coverage Medicaid provides is available at https://www .medicaid.gov/medicaid/ltss/index.html.
- Medicare: This government health insurance program for adults 65 and older only does not cover long-term care costs but will help pay for short-term rehabilitative care in nursing facilities after hospitalization. Information about what Medicare covers is available at https:// www.medicare.gov/.
- Social Security: Your parents can check their Social Security statement and manage their benefits by setting up an online account at https://www.ssa.gov/myaccount/.
- Veterans Affairs: Information about long-term care benefits the VA offers is available at https://www.va.gov/ health-care/about-va-health-benefits/long-term-care/.

SCAMS, FINANCIAL EXPLOITATION, AND IDENTITY THEFT

- AARP Fraud Watch Network: Your parents can sign up to receive scam alerts and report fraud at https://www .aarp.org/fraudwatchnetwork or get fraud counseling by calling 877-908-3360.
- Better Business Bureau: Learn about the latest scams and get tips on avoiding them at https://www.bbb.org/ scamtips.
- Consumer Financial Protection Bureau: This government agency provides a wealth of resources to help consumers protect their finances at https://www.consumer finance.gov/. The CFPB also has a publication, "Money Smart for Older Adults," that offers advice to help prevent financial exploitation of older adults, available at https:// files.consumerfinance.gov/f/201306_cfpb_msoa-partici pant-guide.pdf.
- Federal Trade Commission: This government agency provides scam alerts, or you can browse scams by topic at https://www.consumer.ftc.gov/features/scam-alerts.

- National Adult Protective Services Association: This non-profit organization provides information about financial exploitation, including resource materials and links to state adult protective service agencies to report suspected abuse at http://www.napsa-now.org/.
- National Do Not Call Registry: Your parents can register to stop unwanted sales calls at https://www.donotcall.gov/ or 1-888-382-1222.
- Security and Exchange Commission: This government agency provides resources to protect investors, including "A Guide for Seniors" at https://www.sec.gov/investor/seniors/guideforseniors.pdf

SENIOR HOUSING AND LONG-TERM CARE

- AgingCare: This website provides articles on a variety of aging, senior care, and housing topics and a searchable database to find elder care, senior housing, and caregiver support at https://www.agingcare.com/.
- Aging Life Care Association: This is formerly the National Association of Professional Geriatric Care Managers. Aging life care professionals work with families to coordinate care for older adults, and you can find one through the Aging Life Care Association website at https://www.aginglifecare.org/.
- American Association for Long-Term Care: This association of long-term care insurance professionals provides information about long-term care insurance for consumers. You can get free long-term care insurance quotes from the association's members at https://www.aaltci.org/ or by calling 818-597-3227.
- A Place for Mom: This assisted-living referral service offers guides to senior housing options and tools to search for assisted living, memory care, nursing home, and other senior living options at https://www.aplaceformom.com/.
- Caring.com: This online resource offers articles, tools, and advice about senior living and caregiving options and a directory of caregiving services at https://www.caring.com/.

- Genworth Cost of Care Survey: Insurance company Genworth surveys the costs of various types of long-term care annually. You can calculate the cost of home health care, assisted living, adult day care, and nursing home care in your area by using Genworth's database at https://www.genworth.com/aging-and-you/finances/cost-of-care.html.
- LongTermCare.gov: This U.S. Department of Health and Human Services' website provides information about what long-term care is, who needs it, where to receive care, and how to pay for it at https://longtermcare.acl.gov/.
- National Adult Day Services Association: This association of the adult day services industry provides information about choosing an adult day center and a searchable database to find a center at www.nasda.org. Adult day centers offer health, social, and support services for adults who need supervision and can be an alternative to in-home care.
- Retirement Living Information Center: This online resource provides information on retirement planning and senior living options at https://www.retirementliving.com/.
- SeniorLiving.org: This website offers a directory of senior living options in all 50 states and the District of Columbia and planning resources at https://www.seniorliving.org/. It does not have any direct paid advertising, so it doesn't favor any one service provide over another.
- 55 Places.com: This website offers information about active adult communities and a database to search for communities by state at https://www.55places.com/.
- U.S. Department of Housing and Urban Development: HUD offers housing assistance programs for seniors, including low-rent apartments and housing choice vouchers. Information about federal housing assistance programs for the elderly is available at https://www.hud.gov/topics/information_for_senior_citizens.

About the Author

Author photo by Whitney Williams of Sweet WallyPhotography

Cameron Huddleston is an award-winning journalist with more than 15 years of experience writing about personal finance. She was a contributing editor for Kiplinger.com and wrote the popular Kip Tips column, which was syndicated in Tribune newspapers nationwide. Her work has appeared in *Business Insider, Chicago Tribune, Fortune, Huffington Post, Money, MSN, USA Today,* and many more print and online publications. She has appeared on *Fox & Friends,* MSNBC, and CNN and has been a guest on ABC News Radio, Wall Street Journal Radio, NPR, WTOP in Washington, D.C., KGO in San Francisco, and other personal finance radio shows nationwide. She currently is the Life + Money columnist for GOBankingRates. You can get more of Cameron's easy-to-understand financial advice at CameronHuddleston.com or by following her on Twitter @CHLebedinsky or on Facebook @CameronHuddlestonMoneyExpert.

Acknowledgments

Although I have been a journalist for more than 20 years, I never expected to write a book. The articles I write are typically 1,000 words, so I didn't think I had it in me to put tens of thousands of words down on paper. But I realized that the topic of this book was so important that I couldn't relegate it to just one article, or even a series of articles. So I want to thank everyone who helped make this book possible.

I owe a deep debt of gratitude to Jason Vitug, Erin Lowry, and my agent, Eric Myers of Myers Literary Management, for helping me turn my idea for a book into a reality. Without all of you, there would be no book.

I want to thank Mike Henton of Wiley for taking a chance on me and for patiently shepherding me through the process of getting my first book published. I am grateful to Amy Handy, my copy editor, for taking what I wrote and making it better. And I want to thank the team at Wiley for all of their hard work.

This book wouldn't have been possible without all of the people who took the time to talk with me about conversations they had with their parents. I appreciate your willingness to share your stories with me so that others might learn from your experiences. I also appreciate the financial planners, attorneys, eldercare professionals, and other experts who shared their knowledge with me for this book.

I am grateful to Jeff Bartlett, Cerentha Harris, Katie Wudel, and the team at GOBankingRates for your support and patience while I had to dial back my column writing so I could have enough time to write this book. Thanks for bearing with me.

My deepest thanks to my sister, Robin, who was willing to read every chapter and give me feedback. Your insight as a counselor helped inform me as I tackled the emotional side of having financial conversations with parents. In short, you made sure that I covered a difficult topic with sensitivity. And you encouraged me every step of the way.

Of course, I'm thankful for my children, who cheered me on as I wrote this book. I'm especially thankful to my daughters for keeping their little brother occupied on weekends when I was writing. And I'm eternally grateful to my husband, Alex, for supporting me and for helping care for my mom. I couldn't have done any of this without you.

Finally, thank you to my mom. You'll never read this, but I want you to know how grateful I am to you for always being there for me. I wish Alzheimer's disease hadn't robbed you of your memory and given me a reason to write this book. It is what it is, though. So I hope that in sharing your story – *our story* – I can help other adult children be able to help their parents.

Index